With Faith Like Hers Bible Study Series

I am Rahab

Carol Peterson

Honor Bound Books

Honor Bound Books

Typeset in 12/16/18pt Cambria; cover and title fonts 36 pt Lucinda Handwriting; logo 12ptLucinda Calligraphy. Used with permission from Microsoft. Cover logo font 20 pt Viner Hand ITC, used with permission from Adobe. Cover background and graphics used with permission from Adobe.

ISBN-13: 978-0997778519
ISBN-10: 0997778512

Dedication

This book is dedicated to every woman who thinks God cannot possibly forgive her of her sinful past. It is a reminder that God is less interested in who we were before He came into our lives and more interested in our future with Him.

I am grateful to Pastor Don Bertelsen for his contagious Old Testament enthusiasm, his excellent biblical teaching and for his diligence in reviewing *I am Rahab* through the correcting lens of theology.

Contents

I Can Be Used by God

I Witness

My Future

Preface

It is human nature to explore who we are. It is part of the spiritual journey we take as Christians to explore who we are *in Christ* and seek to understand who God wants us to become. This women's Bible study series focuses on understanding ourselves as Christian women.

Scripture gives us examples of people who lived by faith. They were people just like us—with flaws and foibles; triumphs and turmoil. But they lived a victorious life because they lived in the light of God's love. Outward things have changed since biblical times, but people are basically the same. When we look at the lives of women in Scripture, we glimpse how God saw them. When we learn the lessons they learned, God can show us how He still sees His women today. We can say, "I am like her; I have her faith; I can survive her circumstances. I am she."

That is the basis of the *With Faith Like Hers* series. Each book takes the reader through 28 days of meditative Bible study. We look at a woman in Scripture and see how God—through His Word—viewed her and how He might view our lives in a similar manner. This is Rahab's story. But it is also ours—when we have faith like hers.

Although this book is intended to be an individual daily study, it can also be used effectively as a group study. Simply divide each weekly discussion at the sections—discuss one section each week. Cover day 1 with the first week; cover day 28 with the final week. Some weeks will have fewer days than others, but none will require more than one reading per day. I pray that you will be blessed in your study as you discover how God might see His women of faith.

A Note about Rahab

Throughout the Old and New Testaments, Rahab's name is nearly always attached to her profession—that of a prostitute. Periodically biblical characters were labeled with their profession—Matthew the tax collector, for instance. But after the writers of Scripture had identified those people once, they were simply referred to by their names from then on. Not so with Rahab.

It's as if the writers of Scripture couldn't quite let go of Rahab's profession, continuing to tack her sin onto her whenever they had a chance. Maybe they did so to clearly identify her. Maybe it was to focus on the fact that she had been saved from her sinful past. For whatever reason, when we think of Rahab, we almost always think of her as "Rahab, the prostitute."

Yes, that's what she was. But then she found the God of the Jewish people and her whole life changed. It is because her whole life changed that her life was then recorded in Scripture—pointing to how God redeemed her as an example of how He can redeem us, too.

So what lessons might us modern women learn from a former Old Testament prostitute? Read on. You might very well be surprised!

Day 1—Becoming Rahab

When I first announced I was writing a study about how women can learn lessons about the character and circumstances of Rahab, I got a batch of snickers and a few snide remarks. But as I began to suggest one or two of the lessons I had in mind, people's reactions became, "Hmmm...interesting." Then my husband—always an encouragement about anything biblical—said simply, "Most of us humans prostitute ourselves in some areas of our lives. Men might sell themselves out for success in business. Women might sell themselves out for beauty or weight loss."

Really, how different are those from selling your body for sex—from a spiritual standpoint? Dear Hubby made me think about that for a long time and ultimately I had to agree.

So as we consider the life, character and circumstances of Rahab the prostitute, maybe we can do so with a bit more compassion than we might have initially had. We can open our minds to more possibilities to see her life as a source of lessons—not just how *not* to live, but how to seek to live a better life in this modern world.

The Gospels in our New Testament (the books of Matthew, Mark, Luke and John) are filled with instances when Jesus hung out with "tax collectors and sinners." In fact, He regularly ministered to and forgave prostitutes and other women of "ill repute." We are accustomed to see Jesus in those situations. We don't always expect, however, to see God the Father redeeming prostitutes in the Old Testament.

Rahab is an exception in the Old Testament. Her life was an unusual example of a life redeemed. Her redeemed life, however was also an example of what God regularly does: redeems us and brings us into His family.

The story of Rahab is part of the story of the Jewish people's move from slavery in Egypt to the land promised to them by God. Although entering Canaan was filled with warfare and battle, it nonetheless was a continuation of God's story of grace and redemption of His people.

God owns the entire planet. He can do with it what He determines best. Back in Genesis 15:18, God promised Abraham that the Jewish people (Abraham's descendants through his son Isaac) would occupy the land west of the Jordan River. God had also blessed Abraham's son Ishmael's line in a similar manner, on the condition that they remain true to Him. They didn't; so God determined that the land should be taken from

Ishmael's descendants (in Canaan) and given instead to His chosen people, the Jews through Isaac. The process of Ishmael's line completely falling away from God took 400 years, which is why the Jewish people were in Egypt for that time. Then, when the process of Ishmael's line falling away was completed, God determined that it was time for Isaac's line (the Jewish people) to claim the land.

During the process of claiming the land, God required the Jewish people to cleanse the land of paganism. We meet Rahab at the very beginning of the Jewish people's conquest of Canaan and taking over possession of the land promised to them by God. Right there, Rahab's life became an example of how we Gentiles (non-Jews) can become important in God's plan, even if we weren't born Jewish.

While writing each of these books in the *With Faith Like Hers* Bible study series, God has given me a verse to help me focus. For the writing of this book, God gave me the second half of Joshua 2:11, where Rahab says:

> the LORD your God is God in heaven above
> and on the earth below.

Rahab was a Gentile woman who had little knowledge of Jewish faith, never attended vacation Bible school as a child or listened to an evangelist on TV. As a descendant of Ishmael, she may or may not have heard some of the stories of the God of her ancestor Abraham. She nevertheless understood several important theological truths made clear by this one statement:

The Lord is our God.
The Lord is God in heaven above.
The Lord is God on the earth below.

The story of Rahab is the story of a courageous woman, involved in a battle between her own society and the Jewish people. The story of Rahab is the story of a woman with a sin-filled past who was rescued by God. The story of Rahab is a story of a woman who took on a life-saving faith in the one true God and saved not only herself, but her family and became part of the never-ending life story of our Lord Jesus Himself.

There is not a great deal written about Rahab—no complete book, such as for Esther and Ruth. But there is enough contained in our Holy Bible about Rahab to learn some important lessons from her, based on her character and circumstances. In preparation, please read what is written about Rahab in the following verses:

Joshua 2
Joshua 6:22-25
Matthew 1:1-6
Hebrews 11:31
James 2:25

While reading these verses and throughout our study of Rahab, please keep in mind that Rahab, prostitute though she was, was one of only five women named in Scripture as part of the genealogy of Jesus. This Gentile woman who might have been looked down on by today's society because of her profession, was redeemed by God. She was also loved by God. She was also honored by God, becoming part of God's human lineage, ending in the birth of Jesus.

If Rahab were here she would say this was her story. She lived during a time in history when the Jewish nation was being established, based on a faith in a living God. Rajab chose to be part of that heritage.

Who are we to God? When we realize that although we may not have been born into the Jewish culture, God has brought us into the group of His chosen people when we take on the true faith in Him. Then we can understand how He might see His women of faith. We can respond:

I am like Rahab.

For Thought and Discussion

- Rahab was one of the "bad girls of the Bible." Who else comes to mind? What do you know about those women's faith?

- Do you know someone you consider has "sold themselves" for something in life. How does that make you feel about them?

- In what area of your own life might you consider the possibility that you have "sold yourself" for something? How does that make you feel to think that way?

PRAYER: Dear Jesus, thank you for the people's lives who are recorded in Scripture. Please help us learn the lessons Rahab can teach us. Amen.

I Live in Jericho

Day 2—I Live in a Pagan Society

~~

So often, when we prepare to study Scripture, we need to have some background information. For today's lesson, it is helpful to know a bit about the history of Jericho and the city itself.

The Bible tells us that the Jews destroyed the ancient city of Jericho entirely. Evidently the city was not rebuilt for another 500 years. Archaeologists find buried bits of that rebuilt city, but it is not clear if anything has yet been discovered from the first city spoken about in Scripture. Here are a few things, however, we do know about the first city of Jericho Joshua destroyed.

In Arabic, the name *Jericho* means "city of the moon." It was a walled city. The walls of Jericho however were nothing like the walled European castles we see depicted in movies. Those castle walls typically were a foot or two thick. The walls of Jericho were much wider. Estimates vary, but all assume the walls of Jericho were between 6 feet and 14 feet thick—possibly even wider.

They were also estimated to be over 20 feet high and sat atop an embankment over 40 feet high. Those building facts would have made the city almost impregnable.

Here are verses in Scripture that tell us specifics about the city of Jericho:

- The city was strongly fortified (Joshua 2:5, 7, 15, 6:5, 20).
- The attack occurred just after harvest time in the spring (Joshua 2:6, 3:15, 5:10).
- The inhabitants had no opportunity to flee with their food (Joshua 6:1).
- The siege was short (Joshua 6:15).
- The walls were leveled (Joshua 6:20).
- The city was not plundered (Joshua 6:17-18).
- The city was burned (Joshua 6:20)

Scripture says that Rahab's house was built into or on the wall of Jericho. That fact makes sense once we understand that the wall was perhaps 14 feet wide. Rahab literally made her home as part of the physical structure of the pagan city.

Let's compare what the verses above tell us with how battles would have been conducted during Rahab's time.

First, the walls of Jericho provided strong physical protection for the city. A conquering army could not have simply walked in and taken over. It was not a city sitting in the open. It was not a city protected by a wooden or flimsy stone wall. Jericho's hefty, strongly fortified walls were considered impenetrable. Scripture tells us however, that the city was conquered in seven days.

Secondly, faced with impenetrable walls, a conquering army during that time would normally build a mound against the outside wall, until that mound was high enough to climb over and attack the city. Building that mound with tools of the day would have taken months or years. Scripture tells us the city was conquered in seven days.

Thirdly, Joshua's attack occurred after the harvest. In terms of battle tactics that meant the citizens of Jericho had plenty of food. One war strategy at the time was to starve the people until they surrendered. Starving the food-filled city of Jericho would have been time consuming. Scripture tells us the city was conquered in seven days.

Joshua would have been aware of all of these aspects of trying to conquer Jericho. He knew the walls were impregnable. He knew that normal battle tactics of the time would have required months to wear the city down. But when God told him it would take one week, Joshua had the faith in God's promise to believe.

Looking more closely at Rahab, we know that Rahab's physical home was literally part of the wall of Jericho. She made her home as part of the pagan world the walls encompassed.

Scripture also tells us we are to live in the world but not be of the world.

*The world would love you as one of its own
if you belonged to it, but you are no longer
part of the world. I chose you to come out of
the world, so it hates you* (John 15:19).

In Jericho, Rahab literally lived in the physical structure of the city of her world. She also lived spiritually in that pagan (unbelieving) world until God— through His people—rescued her both physically and spiritually.

People living in Rahab's time often relied on the physical walls of their city to protect them. The people of Jericho would have assumed Jericho couldn't have been won easily by the Jews. But when God was involved and when the Jews followed God's plan, the Jewish people triumphed.

Like everyone in the town of Jericho, Rahab probably had lived her life with a sense of security, imagining the walls would keep enemies out. But she had begun to hear about the power of the God of Abraham. Imagine the faith Rahab must have had to believe that the God of the Jews (her society's enemy) was more powerful than the gods and idols she had grown up worshipping. God must have been hard at work on Rahab's heart. He must also have been hard at work opening her mind to possibilities she might not have considered before.

If Rahab were here she would say this was her story. She lived within the walls of Jericho—a pagan society.

Who are we to God? Like Rahab, we live in a pagan society but are called to not be of it. When we realize that although we sometimes feel secure in our society, we are surrounded by evil and by people who do not know God, we can understand how He might see His women of faith. We can respond:

I am like Rahab.

For Thought and Discussion

- How would living in a city surrounded by 14-foot thick walls affect your sense of security? How physically secure do you feel today?

- Was there ever a time in your life or in history where it was obvious that a battle could not be won or a situation could not be resolved by human hands; but only because God was involved? Explain.

- Is there something you feel God is leading you to do that you feel insecure about doing? How might the example of how God triumphed easily over the fortified city of Jericho give you encouragement to step out in faith?

PRAYER: Dear Jesus, we sing songs about the battle of Jericho and how the walls came tumbling down, but it's hard for us to imagine what a huge event that was at the time. Help us look at our lives and see you at work. Help us allow you to have more power in our own lives. Amen.

Day 3—A Spiritual Wall Separates Me From God

❧❧

Early in my journey of faith, someone drew a little picture to explain how Jesus changed things. On one edge of the page was a cliff labeled "man." On the other edge of the page was drawn a cliff labeled "God." In the center of the gulf was drawn a cross, with the horizontal cross bars bridging the gulf so man could approach God the Father without a spiritual separation.

Man→→→God

I often think about that picture and thank Jesus for making it possible to have a relationship with all three persons of the Trinity because of Jesus' sacrifice on the cross.

Rahab lived in the walled city of Jericho. In fact, her home was physically part of that wall. She likely had a unique view of the city walls and how those walls were a barrier between her and the rest of the world. Physically, those walls separated her and her friends and family from the Jewish people. Physically, those walls separated her from participation in the worship and fellowship with their God.

In addition to the way Jesus bridges a spiritual gap between man and God, another frequent analogy of the separation between God and man is that of a spiritual wall. Although Jesus made the way possible to bridge the gap, sometimes we still put up walls ourselves and try to keep our personal issues away from the "God stuff." These spiritual walls keep us separated from God. Fortunately, Jesus is the way through.

> *Jesus answered, "I am the way and the truth and the life. No one comes to the Father except through me"* (John 14:6).

The walls of Jericho were a physical barrier that separated the people inside from the Jewish people. The walls were both a spiritual and physical wall, separating Rahab from God.

Jesus is the Cornerstone

In architectural engineering, the cornerstone is the first stone laid when a building is constructed. The cornerstone is often larger and stronger than the other stones that make up the foundation. Thus, every other stone of the foundation, and in fact the whole building itself, relies on the strength of the cornerstone. Jesus—and our trust in Him—is the cornerstone of our faith. Every other part of our faith; indeed, of our lives rests on Him.

> *This Jesus is the stone that was rejected by you, the builders, which has become the cornerstone* (also the *capstone;* Acts 4:11; see also Isaiah 28:16, Luke 20:17, Mark 12:10, Psalm 118:22, Ephesians 2:20, Matthew 21:42, Zechariah 10:4).

The cornerstone of a building also determines the relationship to every other stone in the foundation. All other stones in the foundation are set in relation to that first stone. Thus the position of the entire structure is determined by the position of the cornerstone.

The Jewish people before Jesus relied on following laws and doing good work to be considered righteous. Then Jesus came.

Jesus knew that even the Pharisees who focused on following laws and doing the proper things, could not be saved by their own actions. Only Jesus' sacrifice can save us, provide for our forgiveness and be the true foundation for our faith. Paul reminds us of this in Romans:

> *But now apart from the law the righteousness of God has been made known, to which the Law and the Prophets testify. This righteousness is given through faith in Jesus Christ to all who believe. There is no difference between Jew and Gentile, for all have sinned and fall short of the glory of God, and all are justified freely by his grace through the redemption that came by Christ Jesus* (Romans 3:21-24).

Jesus is the cornerstone of our faith upon which everything else is built. He is our strong foundation. The walls of Jericho were built into the foundation of the city. Every part of that city was built on or within those walls. But spiritually, the city of Jericho was not built upon faith in God. And the city fell. Similarly, throughout the Bible, we are shown that if our actions are not based on faith, they will often fail.

Jesus is the Gate

In our faith, there may be spiritual walls that separate us from Jesus, but Jesus tells us that there is a there is a gate.

> *I am the gate; whoever enters through me will be saved. They will come in and go out, and find pasture* (John 10:9).

Rahab made her home as part of the walls of Jericho, possibly even near the city gate. She would have known who was coming and going. She would have watched what was happening. Her establishment was a hub—not for the righteous perhaps, but nonetheless, she knew folks.

When it came to living at the spiritual town gate, Rahab was spiritually right there where she could walk through the gate. Although the Jews in Rahab's time only looked ahead to a day when Jesus would come, spiritually Rahab also lived in faith toward Jesus' coming when she took on the faith of the Jews. Rahab thus passed through Jesus' spiritual gate to physically exit Jericho and spiritually enter the Kingdom of Heaven.

Jesus is at the Door

The books of Matthew and Revelation both mention a door to salvation. They both also indicate that we are on one side of the door and Jesus is on the other side.

> *"Ask and it will be given to you; seek and you will find; knock and the door will be opened to you. For everyone who asks receives; the one who seeks finds; and to the one who knocks, the door will be opened"* (Matthew 7:7-8).

> *"Here I am! I stand at the door and knock. If anyone hears my voice and opens the door, I will come in and eat with that person, and they with me"* (Revelation 3:20).

In Matthew, Jesus expects us to knock. In Revelation, Jesus is doing the knocking. The point is that there is a door; Jesus is there and He wants it to open so that we can both be on the same side of the door.

The very first and the very last books of the New Testament tell us there is a door. The rest of the books of the New Testament in between the first and the last tell us about Jesus and what to expect when that door is open.

Rahab literally lived within the walls of Jericho. That wall separated her from the people who worshipped the one true God. But Rahab found a way to go beyond the walls that kept her inside. Spiritually, she opened the door and walked through in faith.

When we recognize the truth that Jesus is the cornerstone, the gate and is at the door of our heart waiting for us to join Him, we understand how God might see His women of faith. We can respond:

I am like Rahab.

For Thought and Discussion

- What type of foundation do you have in your home? Is it set on a wall of concrete or cement blocks? Is it a slab poured onto the ground with deeper concrete footings? How might you think about the security of your home and relate it to Jesus as the foundation of our faith?

- Today cornerstones laid in buildings are often ceremonial or decorative with the date and building name stamped into the stone. How might we use the idea of having a decorative cornerstone on our house to share Jesus with the world?

- Which symbol—the cornerstone, gate or door—best describes Jesus to you? How can you use that imagery to better keep Jesus in your thinking throughout the day?

PRAYER: Dear Jesus, thank you for making it possible for us to breach the walls separating us from you. Thank you for the many parables you have given us in Scripture to describe yourself. Please help us seek new ways to find you each day. Amen.

Day 4—A Spiritual Wall Protects Me

I love praying for people I love and asking Jesus to send guardian angels to protect them.

> *The angel of the Lord encamps around those who fear him, and he delivers them* (Psalm 34:7).

Angels may be one of the greatest protective blessings we have. Angels are beings created by God to do His will. Fortunately, one of the things on His "will list" is to protect His people from evil.

Similarly, I also love praying a hedge of protection around them as taught by Job.

> *"Have you not put a hedge around him and his household and everything he has? You have blessed the work of his hands, so that*

his flocks and herds are spread throughout the land" (Job 1:10).

The idea in Job that God builds a hedge or wall around us to protect us gives us a sense of security. Throughout Scripture are stories and parables of people who built hedges, walls and watchtowers to protect their crops. When Jesus refers to believers as a harvest, and relates how we receive the Gospel (the good seed) depending on the type of spiritual soil we are, the idea of a protective wall is especially meaningful.

Earlier we discussed the fact that we live in a pagan (unbelieving) society, just as Rahab did in Jericho. We also saw that the physical wall of Jericho was a physical barrier keeping the people inside the city from knowing God. A further lesson we can learn from Rahab about her circumstances living within the walls of Jericho is that, just as God—through the spies—protected Rahab and those in her house from destruction, so too does Jesus protect us who believe in Him. God built a spiritual wall of protection around Rahab.

> *The Lord is my light and my salvation—so why should I be afraid? The Lord is my fortress, protecting me from danger, so why should I tremble?* (Psalm 27:1)

Before Rahab ever heard about the God of the Jewish people, she probably felt safe and secure within those formidable walls of Jericho. They were strong and mighty and impossible to conquer. But once the army of

God demolished the city walls, she became aware that those *physical walls* were no protection at all.

Fortunately, when Rahab left the perceived security of the city of Jericho, she then came under the protection and security of God. Although she saw the walls of Jericho fall, she knew God's protection was far more powerful. She had come under the protection of God's *spiritual* walls.

This is Rahab's story. Rahab learned that God is stronger than any stone walls. His security is stronger than the evil one. His spiritual security is all our eternal souls need. Ever.

When we recognize that—through Jesus—we are spiritually secure forever, we understand how God might see His women of faith. We can respond:

I am like Rahab.

For Thought and Discussion

- How do you rely on God for physical security?

- How do you rely on God for spiritual security?

- Which of the Scriptures cited today (or another one) gives you the greatest sense of spiritual and/or physical security? Why?

PRAYER: Dear Jesus, thank you for loving us enough to want to keep us safe. Thank you for promising that our souls are eternally safe with you. Thank you for the promise that—even though this world is filled with evil—one day we will be with you in heaven where we will never know evil again. Amen.

Day 5—Some Days I feel Trapped

≈∂

When my son was born, my husband and I had just moved to the other side of the country. I knew no one, there was no Facebook (or Internet at all). The snow and cold of the east coast winter kept me and my newborn locked inside the house. With my husband traveling for work, many days I felt trapped.

We've talked about how the ancient city of Jericho might represent spiritual walls that separate us from God. We've also talked about how they might represent God's protection of us. In our modern world, harsh winter weather can give folks cabin fever. Being sick for weeks can make us long for fresh air. Sometimes, walls that surround us also make us feel trapped.

What would it have felt like for Rahab to live within the walls of Jericho? What would her life have felt like to live in her new home outside those walls, with the

Jews? Was there a sense of freedom she found once she left Jericho?

We know the site of the ancient city of Jericho was located on a major travel route. There was one "highway" going north and south and another going east and west. Both highways intersected at Jericho. That meant the city was bustling and busy. People were always coming and going. It was a lively trade center; a hub of business.

But with all the coming and going, the people of Jericho—especially Rahab—probably were not among those traveling. They stayed put and offered their supplies and services to the people passing through.

Because Jericho was such a busy city, it was probably also a place where new ideas took hold as other cultures traveling through the city brought their practices and beliefs with them.

In our world today, travel, relocation and technology mean that every new idea can reach us. We can no longer easily insulate ourselves and our families from ideas and people who are not of God.

When I was growing up, the half-hour sitcom was king of evening television. Those TV shows did not contain graphic language or graphic scenes. Parents didn't need to shield us from watching those programs. They were all pretty neutral, if not downright uplifting spiritually.

Fast forward to today. TV shows contain characters who wear cross jewelry but kill arbitrarily. Families are gender whatever. Sex with anybody and everybody is not only natural, but to be sought, regardless of any consequences that would happen in the real world.

It's hard to shield our children and ourselves from ideas and beliefs that could take us away from the path Jesus has in mind for us. It is hard to get away from unwanted ideas that are not of God when all of society is filled with those ideas. Many days we can feel trapped inside a society where evil can focus its attention on us.

> *The thief's purpose is to steal and kill and destroy. My purpose is to give them a rich and satisfying life* (John 10:10).

> *For I know the plans I have for you," says the Lord. "They are plans for good and not for disaster, to give you a future and a hope* (Jeremiah 29:11).

Rahab literally lived within the walls of Jericho. But those walls did not protect her from the people who traveled through Jericho, bringing new and different ideas into her culture. Although the news of the God of the Jewish people was a good thing that came to her from outside the walls, Rahab would have had to have been on guard against other beliefs passing through her town. She would have had to have had wisdom to discern what was evil from what was good for her and her family. Evidently Rahab *did* have that wisdom.

When we recognize how we also must be wary of ideas and beliefs that could lead us away from God, we understand how God might see His women of faith. We can respond:

I am like Rahab.

For Thought and Discussion

- Did you have a favorite book or TV show as a child that was uplifting or encouraged your faith in Christ? How did it do that?

- What do you especially need to guard your family and yourself against in terms of ideas or beliefs that you feel lead you away from Christ or into temptation?

- What is the biggest or most effective thing you can do to protect yourself and your family from destructive ideas from within our society?

PRAYER: Dear Jesus, thank you for promising to protect us from evil. Please give us wisdom to understand when what society says may be leading us away from you and toward temptation or outright evil. Help us be strong and help us first rely on you for strength and protection. Amen.

There is a Battle

Day 6—Spiritual Battle Surrounds Me

One of the things I regularly thank God for is for *not* being able to see what is happening in the spiritual world. One day, when we're sitting up in heaven, we'll probably be able to see what's going on. But for now, I'm grateful I can't. Whenever an angel shows up in Scripture, the first thing he says to the hapless human is "Do not be afraid." Imagine being able to see demons, too.

In Rahab's time, we know that one of God's angels showed up for at least Joshua to see. God had told Joshua to go and conquer Jericho so the land of Canaan could be cleansed from idolatry and the Jewish people could take ownership of it. We see this angel show up before the battle.

> *When Joshua was near the town of Jericho, he looked up and saw a man standing in front of him with sword in hand. Joshua*

went up to him and demanded, "Are you friend or foe?"

Neither one," he replied. "I am the commander of the Lord's army."

At this, Joshua fell with his face to the ground in reverence. "I am at your command," Joshua said. "What do you want your servant to do?"

The commander of the Lord's army replied, "Take off your sandals, for the place where you are standing is holy." And Joshua did as he was told (Joshua 5:13-15).

This angel wasn't one of those we might see on a Christmas card—with flowing blond hair and wispy wings. This angel was the commander of God's army. The *Commander.* Of God's *army. God's* army.

And the first thing the angel commander told Joshua to do? Recognize the holiness that being in the presence of God's messenger implied.

This passage points out the fact that God has an army. It points out that God's angels represent God's holiness. It points out another amazing time that a mere mortal was given the gift of seeing one of God's spiritual beings.

This passage also is a reminder that God has a plan to protect His people from evil and to further His spiritual plan. It also reminds us that there is a spiritual battle going on. If there were no spiritual battle, God wouldn't need a spiritual army. He certainly wouldn't need a spiritual army commander.

Rahab clearly knew that the army of the Jewish people belonged to God. She may have even been looking out her window on the wall and saw the angel commander. She knew that God's army was fighting. At some level, she knew it would be a spiritual battle.

Scripture regularly indicates that our souls are always in danger. Here are a few verses of Scripture that remind us of the battle God is fighting for our souls.

> *Be alert and of sober mind. Your enemy the devil prowls around like a roaring lion looking for someone to devour* (1 Peter 5:8).

> *Submit yourselves, then, to God. Resist the devil, and he will flee from you* (James 4:7).

> *For he has rescued us from the dominion of darkness and brought us into the kingdom of the Son he loves* (Colossians 1:13).

I'm happy not to be able to see the battle going on around me—even though I know the battle is God's and that He will win.

This is Rahab's story. We might wonder if Rahab, looking out the window of her home within the wall of Jericho could have spotted the commander of the Lord's army. Even if she had not seen him, she later probably heard the story about the angelic encounter, and ultimately understood the truth of the spiritual battle led by the God of the Jewish people.

When we recognize the truth that although God shields our vision from the battle around us, the battle is still going on and that Jesus shields us spiritually and protects us from evil, we understand how God might see His women of faith. We can respond:

I am like Rahab.

For Thought and Discussion

- Would seeing the spiritual battle around you increase your faith, knowing the truth of what Jesus says by having seen it with your own eyes?

- What is the difference between knowing something because you can see or touch it and having faith? Which feels stronger to you?

- Is there any aspect of your life you might give over to God so He could fight the battle for you? Health, temptation, relationships?

PRAYER: Dear Jesus, thank you for protecting us from evil. Thank you for being stronger than the enemy. Thank you for your promise that you will win the battle and that we remain yours. Amen.

Day 7—God's Way Is Not Man's Way

ॐॐ

O ne of my favorite sayings is: If you want to make God laugh, just tell Him your plan.

Often we decide on a course of action we want to take. Then we ask God to bless our plan. Sometimes that's OK because sometimes our plan happens to also be God's plan. Or sometimes our plan at least doesn't conflict with God's plan so He allows it to be fulfilled through His permissive will.

Sometimes though, it becomes clear either very quickly or after a great length of time that our plan is *not* what God has in mind. Ultimately when God moves and His plan is accomplished we can look back and see His hand and thank Him for not allowing our idea to move forward.

Other times we reach the same end, but how we thought we'd get there and the route God took us look nothing like each other. Sometimes it's as if God is showing off a bit, saying: "See what I can do? Just in case you forgot."

The Jewish people were pretty smart. They had people who had studied the art of war. They knew how to make battle plans and they knew when and how to do what and where. In fact, Numbers 21:14 references *The Book of the Wars of the Lord*. Although that book has been lost over the millennia, its existence indicates that not only did the Jewish people understand war, they studied it. They recorded it. They knew what they were doing.

The Jewish army officers probably started out with a standard battle plan when they looked at Jericho. But then, God intervened and told the Jews He had a different battle plan; a different way to win the war.

No human would be likely to think up a way to conquer a city like God did. God told the Jewish people to march around the city walls, shouting and playing trumpets. Basically, God planned to conquer Jericho with music and shouts of praise.

There are at least two points for us to remember about this:

First, God's commands, even when they seem foolish, bring victory through faith and obedience. The Israelites had faith in God. They knew God kept His promises to them. They had a history where God told them what to do. When they obeyed, God was victorious and they prospered. When He told them to do something and they didn't, well, then, sometimes they spent the next 40 years meandering about the desert.

Rahab had fledgling faith in God. She had heard about God and the things He had done for His people. But perhaps she didn't have firsthand experience seeing His promises kept. When she offered to help the spies, God had not yet told them His battle plan. We might wonder if she had known that the plan was for the Israelite army to march around the city for seven days playing music— would she have been as trusting that God would win the battle?

The point is not what she knew or what she thought personally about God's battle plan. The point is that before the battle began, Rahab put her trust in God. Then—no matter how wacky the plan sounded to human ears—Rahab watched as He was victorious. Can you imagine how Rahab's faith must have blossomed to watch what God did and how He did it and saw that the result was victory in battle?

How much more must her faith have grown to watch as God fulfilled His people's promise to her and her family personally.

Second, God's battle plan teaches us that there is power in praise. There have been many times in my life where I have felt incapable of handling whatever was happening in my life. On some of those occasions, I admit that I either delved deeply into despair or at the very least self-pity. Oh, woe. How can I? How did this? How will I?

But other times, I have taken the Apostle Paul's advice to heart and looked at my circumstances with gratitude.

When my mother-in-law was dying, I had the opportunity to attend to her physical care. I felt incapable. I didn't think I had the strength to do what was needed. Emotionally I didn't want to be so close to the situation that I would be forced to watch my beloved mother-in-law leave this earth through physical suffering. Physically I didn't think I could handle the trauma of dealing with end of life care.

But when I began the task first praising God and thanking Him for her life and the many people's lives she touched; when I praised God for the legacy of faith she was leaving behind through her family; when I praised God for her example of her love for Jesus, then I found the power I needed to care for her in a way that might ease her out of this life and into eternity with her Savior.

I was able to accomplish what I was incapable of accomplishing through my own strength, because I first began with praise.

There is power in praise. Think of the praise Rahab would have had, when—knowing the Jewish army was about to attack her city—the spies promised to save her and her family. Imagine the strength that promise gave Rahab to do what she needed to do in the threat of war.

This is Rahab's story. Rahab had planned a regular, normal day before the spies arrived. Then God changed her plans. She may not have known how God planned to win the battle. She trusted in God's victory though and her faith was strengthened as He kept His promise to her and her family, made through the spies.

When we recognize that God's plan is better than whatever we might come up with on our own, and when we trust in His perfect plan for our lives, beginning with praise for Him, we understand how God might see His women of faith. We can respond:

I am like Rahab.

For Thought and Discussion

- Has there been a time when you asked God to bless your plan and He did? Do you believe it might have been His plan also? Or was allowing it part of His permissive will for your life?

- Has there been a time when you asked God to bless your plan and He clearly said "no"? What was the result? Did you see that His plan was clearly better? If not, are you asking Him for understanding?

- Is there something you sense God leading you to do that feels outside your ability or comfort zone? How might you first begin with praise?

PRAYER: Dear Jesus, thank you for knowing everything. Thank you for showing us your creativity in creation and in everything you do. Help us trust in your power to accomplish things through us, even if we don't understand the "how" at the time. Help us remember to praise you in all circumstances and to find your power in that praise. Amen.

Day 8—I Participate in God's Battle

❧

O ne of my all-time favorite hymns is *Onward Christian Soldier*. When I was little, I'd sing that hymn with as much gusto as a child could. But I never truly understood what the Christian faith of love had to do with soldiers.

It wasn't really until I became a Bible-studying adult that I understood the truth of the spiritual battle going on around me and that—even though God shields us from seeing it—He expects us to participate in it to the extent we are able.

Rahab realized that the battle for the city of Jericho was God's battle. God's battle plan included obedience and praise and God even sent the commander of His army to lead Joshua and the Jews into battle.

Rahab too participated in the battle for Jericho. She took sides in the battle for her city, working for the Jewish spies. She was no longer a bystander. Rather, she became a traitor to her own people. Although she stayed within the city while the battle was going on outside the walls, she was nonetheless on the battle front—on God's side.

Today, we still have a responsibility to participate in God's battle. Fortunately, God doesn't expect us to toss grenades at demons or fight hand-to-hand with Satan. But God does expect us to notice when evil is present and to stand up and speak out for God. Or at the very least, God expects us to pray in intercession for God's plan to succeed and for God's people to be protected and strengthened.

God also expects us to participate in the battle by acknowledging first that the battle exists and that it is a danger to our souls. Additionally, God expects us to help provide for our own protection by putting on His spiritual armor. If it is difficult for us to know when to put on His armor then we can wear His armor at all times so that we are always prepared.

Throughout Scripture we are told to wear Christ's robe of righteousness. We are to clothe ourselves in truth. And specifically, the Apostle Paul tells us to wear spiritual armor. (See Ephesians 6:10:18)

Spiritual armor includes the belt of truth—Jesus—which can hold us together. The breastplate of righteousness can protect our heart. We can wear the Gospel of peace like shoes as we walk confidently into the world and share Jesus with others peacefully. Our faith can shield us from Satan's arrows flinging about us. We can protect our right thinking by wearing salvation like a helmet. Our sword is the word of God which can be used both as defensively and offensively.

Rahab expected the Jewish people to be victorious in the battle for Jericho because she had heard the stories of what their God had done for them in the past.

Then Rahab took action on behalf of God's battle. She risked her own life to save members of God's army. She participated in God's battle.

When we realize that God is at war with evil and that the battle is going on around us at all times, and when we take part in that battle, standing up for God and taking steps to protect ourselves with the armor He has provided, then we understand how God might see His women of faith. We can respond,

I am like Rahab.

For Thought and Discussion

- What evidence do you see of a spiritual battle going on around you? Do you regularly take God's side when you see evil prospering?

- Do you daily put on God's armor? In what way might you be better reminded to do so?

- Which piece of God's armor feels most important to you? Which piece might you need to focus more on?

PRAYER: Thank you Jesus for fighting a spiritual battle on our behalf. Thank you for your protection from evil. Please remind us to put on your armor each day and help us find ways to encourage others to put on your armor, too. Amen.

Day 9—I Claim God's Victory

಄ഌ

Even though I was raised in a Christian home, ultimately I had to make a decision on my own to accept Jesus. One of the troubles I had in getting to that point was the idea of surrendering my life to Jesus.

"Wait a minute," I'd say to myself. "Jesus made me to be a strong and independent woman," I reasoned. "It doesn't make sense He would make me strong and independent and then ask me to surrender my will to His."

Ultimately I got the point.

Sometimes my will is good. Jesus' will however is not just good, but perfect. Always. Why in heavens would I want to settle for good sometimes when I can have perfect always?

In other words, Jesus has done all the work. The spiritual battle belongs to Him. All I have to do is claim His victory. Jesus won. By choosing Jesus, I win, too.

The great thing about the Book of Revelation is that God tells us in no uncertain terms that God wins the battle against Satan. Still, you can read the Book of Revelation a dozen times before you get over the horror of what is to come and start celebrating the victory. Jesus has already been victorious over death. He has already won the battle. By choosing Jesus, I win, too. I can claim God's victory.

> *Joshua spared Rahab the prostitute, with her family and all who belonged to her, because she hid the men Joshua had sent as spies to Jericho—and she lives among the Israelites to this day* (Joshua 5:25).

Scripture tells us that after the battle, Rahab went to live with the Jewish people. Through other Scripture referring to Rahab as "righteous" and naming her in the genealogy of Jesus, we know that she claimed the Jewish faith as her own. In doing so, she claimed God's spiritual victory promised to the Jews through the Messiah to come, Jesus.

In Rahab's time, the world concluded that a victory in battle meant a victory for the people's god. When Rahab heard about the Israelites, she heard about the power of their God, saying

When we heard of it, our hearts melted in fear and everyone's courage failed because of you, for the Lord your God is God in heaven above and on the earth below (Joshua 2:11).

Scripture often refers to battles as belonging to God. In the Old Testament, the Spirit of the Lord came upon Jahaziel son of Zechariah who told King Jehoshaphat:

But you will not even need to fight. Take your positions; then stand still and watch the Lord's victory. He is with you, O people of Judah and Jerusalem. Do not be afraid or discouraged. Go out against them tomorrow, for the Lord is with you!" (2 Chronicles 20:17).

When Pharaoh was chasing the Jewish slaves as they escaped Egypt, Moses told them:

The Lord himself will fight for you. Just stay calm" (Exodus 14:14).

When David went out to battle Goliath:

And everyone assembled here will know that the LORD rescues his people, but not with sword and spear. This is the LORD's battle, and he will give you to us!" (1 Samuel 17:47)

Other Scripture assures us that even if we are the ones doing the battling, we have God working in and through us. The battle still belongs to Him.

But you belong to God, my dear children. You have already won a victory over those people, because the Spirit who lives in you is greater than the spirit who lives in the world (1 John 4:4).

For every child of God defeats this evil world, and we achieve this victory through our faith. And who can win this battle against the world? Only those who believe that Jesus is the Son of God (1 John 5:4-5).

What shall we say about such wonderful things as these? If God is for us, who can ever be against us? (Romans 8:31)

Again and again, Scripture reminds us that it is God who is battling evil, and winning every time. It is also God, through Jesus' sacrifice and leaving us with the Holy Spirit, who empowers us to participate in His victory. God's side is the winning side. Have we chosen to be on His victorious side in the spiritual battle against evil?

God who knows everything that has ever happened and who knows everything that will ever happened has already told us the ending to His plan. He wins. God wins because He is fighting Satan. Satan fights in order to turn people away from God. But Satan was merely created by God Himself and will never have the power that God has. Satan therefore has no hope of ultimate victory in the battle.

God wins. God has told us He wins. As God's people, we share in God's victory.

Satan and people who belong to him, have no hope. They only have reason for their hearts to melt in fear and for their courage to fail them. For our God, is the God in heaven above and here on earth. Forever.

This is Rahab's story. She had heard what God had done and she knew He would be victorious. She trusted that God would win the battle because she trusted in His power. She then chose to claim His victory as her own.

When we realize and remember that God will be victorious and trust in His victory to come, we understand how God might see His women of faith. We can respond:

I am like Rahab.

For Thought and Discussion

- What victory has God achieved that you claim? What were the circumstances when you claimed it?

- What victory that God has achieved have you not yet claimed in your life? How can you claim it?

- Is there a victory in your life you want God to achieve? Have you asked Him to fight the battle for you?

PRAYER: Dear Jesus, thank you for fighting for us. Thank you for protecting us from evil and keeping us safe spiritually. Thank you also for the assurances in Scripture that you will be victorious over evil and for promising that we will be safe forever with you in Heaven. Please help us always come to you first when we struggle. Help us release our hold on our battles and let you fight them for us. Amen.

My Character

Day 10—I am Courageous

࿔

Some days I'm such a wimp. I'm afraid of spiders that wiggle and squish. I'm afraid to bite into a potentially wormy apple. I'm afraid of zombies because obviously I watch too many B-rated movies.

I'm also afraid of things I should be afraid of: terrorists, driving icy mountain roads; Satan and his minions. I'm only courageous at all because I trust that God is in control. Even if I die, I know God will take me safely home where I'll live with Him forever away from terrorism, danger and evil.

The thing about courage is, that it is only ever present when there is danger or fear. Courage is about acting—doing the right or necessary thing—despite the danger or fear.

Basically, Rahab was a spy during wartime. Yes, the Jews told her she and her family would be protected, but there must have been some doubt in her mind. Was she doing the right thing? Would her family really be safe? Would the Jewish men really keep their word? Did they even have the authority to make her that promise?

We know Rahab was afraid. She even told the spies that all of her people were afraid.

> *We have heard how the Lord dried up the water of the Red Sea for you when you came out of Egypt, and what you did to Sihon and Og, the two kings of the Amorites east of the Jordan, whom you completely destroyed. When we heard of it, our hearts melted in fear and everyone's courage failed because of you* (Joshua 2:10-11).

As a spy, Rahab faced death from her government for harboring the Jewish spies. If they found out she had lied to them, the king would have killed her instantly. Certainly she must have been afraid. But even though Rahab was afraid, she also believed that the God of the Jews would prevail. She knew, as she said, that

> *the Lord your God is God in heaven above and on the earth below* (Joshua 2:11).

We know that God will ultimately prevail in the spiritual battle. The Book of Revelation tells us that when Jesus returns, there will be a final spiritual battle. But, praise God, He wins.

We have the assurance that God wins because of His Word in Scripture. We can trust the Word of God because we can trust Him. Therefore we can take courage in our trust, knowing God will prevail.

Additionally, we have Paul's words to the church at Philippi, where he assures us:

I can do all this through him who gives me strength (Philippians 4:13).

Our strength from Christ results in strength of faith; strength of will; strength of body. It can result in courage, even when the situation is otherwise filled with danger or fear.

When Rahab hid the spies, she sent the king's men on a false trail to enable the spies to report back to Joshua. Rahab displayed courage and willingness to risk her own life for a bigger purpose. When the spies told her she would not be saved if she betrayed them. She responded, saying

"I accept your terms," she replied. And she sent them on their way, leaving the scarlet rope hanging from the window (Joshua 2:21).

This is Rahab's story. She knew she faced death at the hands of her government if the king learned she had helped the spies. She also knew she faced death at the hands of the Jews if she betrayed them. And she knew it would have been easy for the spies to gain her help and then betray her afterwards.

Rahab would have recognized that she was placing her family's lives on the line based on the word of strangers. Rahab had heard about the faith of the Jewish people though and how they lived according to that faith. When she adopted their faith, she found courage amid overwhelming odds.

When we recognize that God grants us courage amid overwhelming odds and gives us strength when we call upon the name of Jesus, we understand how God might see His women of faith. We can respond:

I am like Rahab.

For Thought and Discussion

- What are some of your common fears? Are they irrational or founded on experience or fact?

- What deeper spiritual fears do you have? How do you rely on Jesus for strength to face them?

- What fears have you not yet faced that God might be calling you to face? How can you ask Him to help you face and overcome them?

PRAYER: Dear Jesus, thank you for your strength. Thank you also for making your strength available to us through the Holy Spirit. Please, Holy Spirit, help us attune our minds and hearts to your leading so that you can help us face and overcome our fears. Please remind us Jesus that you have overcome death and that you have been victorious over evil. Amen.

Day 11—I Know What to Keep Secret

❧⧏

Sometimes I lie. I tell my friend I like her new hairdo when I actually don't think it flatters her. I tell people I am great on days when I want to go home and lock out the world. I almost titled this Day *I Know When to Lie*. I liked the idea of giving you readers a little shock.

Basically, Rahab lied to the King of Jericho. He asked if she knew where the spies were. She flat out told the King's men:

> But the woman had taken the two men and hidden them. She said, "Yes, the men came to me, but I did not know where they had come from. At dusk, when it was time to close the city gate, **they left. I don't know which way they went.** Go after them quickly. You may catch up with them." (But she had taken them up to the roof and hidden them under the stalks of flax she had

laid out on the roof.) (Joshua 2:4-6, emphasis added).

Rahab knew exactly where the spies were. They hadn't left yet. They were upstairs. Rahab lied to the King.

There are many verses of Scripture that tell us not to lie. Here are a few.

> *Do not lie to each other, since you have taken off your old self with its practices and have put on the new self, which is being renewed in knowledge in the image of its Creator* (Colossians 3:9-10).

> *Do not testify against your neighbor without cause—would you use your lips to mislead?* (Proverbs 24:28).

> *Do not steal. Do not lie. Do not deceive one another* (Leviticus 19:11).

God wants us to be truthful. However, there are times in Scripture when God seems to approve of or even suggest that one of His faithful lie. For example, when God tells Samuel to go to Bethlehem to find David. Samuel replies

> *"How can I do that? If Saul hears about it, he will kill me."*

> *"Take a heifer with you," the Lord replied, "and say that you have come to make a sacrifice to the Lord (1 Samuel 16:2).*

Basically, God told Samuel to lie; or at the very least to withhold the truth from King Saul. That lie protected Samuel and saved his life. It also enabled God's plan of anointing King David to be fulfilled.

People often quote the Ten Commandments as saying it is a sin to lie. In reality, number nine of the Ten Commandments says it is a sin to "bear false witness against your neighbor."

> *You shall not give false testimony against your neighbor* (Exodus 20:16).

Just like there are rules in the court that a witness must tell the truth when testifying, Commandment number nine is God's law that says when witnessing, especially when witnessing against your neighbor, God wants us to be entirely truthful. What hangs in the balance is a judgment against someone.

We are never to bear false witness—never to testify or give evidence of something against another person that would result in an innocent person being judged guilty.

The result of bearing false witness could cause injustice. Our just God seeks justice in all instances. Therefore, we are to testify truthfully as it relates to other people and leave the judgment to God in His timing.

God is very clear about our relationships with each other. We are to play nicely. We are not to deal falsely. The basis of the ninth commandment is about our relationships with each other. When Jesus came, He clearly told us that the number two most important thing to do—after loving God—is to love others. Our faith is to include having good relationships with other people.

> *Therefore each of you must put off falsehood and speak truthfully to your neighbor, for we are all members of one body* (Ephesians 4:25).

God also wants others to look upon His children and see a bit of Him. How much of a witness (there's that courtroom jargon again) would we be if we were known as liars?

This emphasis on false testimony does not mean we have an "out" that gives us a license to lie any time we want. We do not. We do *not*. Again and again, Scripture tells us that God does not want us to lie. But right here in Joshua, we see an instance where the focus is less on lying and more on the latter part of Proverbs 12:22:

> *The Lord detests lying lips, but* **he delights in people who are trustworthy** (emphasis added)

Some versions of Proverbs 12:22 say "God delights in people who act faithfully," which nicely fits with what Rahab did. She lied in order to act faithfully for God. Looking at Rahab's actions in light of Proverbs:

- God probably *detested* that Rahab lied but
- He probably *delighted* that Rahab acted faithfully.

- God then rewarded her for acting faithfully, by honoring her life and including her in Jesus' genealogy.

We wonder if God looks at the heart and sees that sometimes the reason for the lie is important—maybe even a righteous reason. James referred to Rahab as "right with God" even though he knew she had lied.

> *Rahab the prostitute is another example. She was shown to be right with God **by her actions** when she hid those messengers and sent them safely away by a different road* (James 2:25; emphasis added).

Rahab lied, but her actions were judged right with God because she acted in order to protect God's people and His plan. She did not falsely testify about the spies in a way that would have caused them to be judged wrongly. The situation was not a matter of injustice. Rather what she did was done to protect God's plan and His people.

If you had lived in Nazi Germany and the Gestapo came to your house you might lie to protect any Jews hiding in your home. Similarly, under the rules of war, Rahab might have been judged innocent by God for lying to the King's men to protect the Jews hiding in her home.

When we look at the situation from God's perspective, Rahab is commended for the faith she had and her strength of conviction in believing that God is righteous. It was her faith that was important in God's eyes. Her faith demanded that she protect God's people.

Rahab may not have been raised to value truth in all circumstances. But she knew that during a time of war, she had to take upon herself the protection of God's people. Her actions were based on her faith in God.

One more thought relating to the title of today's meditation. We should absolutely pay attention and know when to keep things secret that are told to us in confidence. Participating in and spreading gossip can be the cause of many interpersonal battles in our lives. We should have nothing to do with gossip—not starting it, not strengthening it, not even listening to it. We should know what to keep secret in order to protect others.

This was Rahab's story. Because of her actions—including lying to the King—God commended her for her faith and honored her by recording her life in Scripture. She knew what to keep secret.

When we realize that God insists on truth when it comes to our relationship with Him and others, but that protection of His people and plan are also of great importance, we understand how He might see His women of faith. We can respond:

I am like Rahab.

For Thought and Discussion

- Explain the difference between a lie and bearing false witness. If God wants us to witness our faith to others, how might *not* sharing Jesus be like bearing false witness?

- Can you think of any instance when God would consider lying as acting faithfully for Him? What is your opinion of the Scriptural instances discussed here?

- How is spreading gossip different from or like lying? Is telling the truth OK if the result is harm to someone else? How do you keep confidences when someone specifically asks you a question?

PRAYER: Dear Jesus, it's sometimes hard to do everything in a way that pleases you. Please give us clear discernment in our dealings with other people. Help us always act in a manner that lifts others up and shines your light through what we say and do. Amen.

Day 12—I am Considered Righteous

❧

Scripture tells us that Rahab was judged righteous by her actions. But then we look at Ecclesiastes:

> *Indeed, there is no one on earth who is righteous, no one who does what is right and never sins* (Ecclesiastes 7:20).

Ouch. Speaking from personal experience, why is it so easy to be *self righteous* and so hard to get the *self* out of the way and just be *righteous?*

Rahab had been born into a pagan society. She had heard stories of the Jews and their God, but she probably had no training in their faith. She did not understand the commandments God had set out as a way for His people to live. She was a grown adult when she became part of the Jewish society. She might have been a "good" person despite her occupation. But she probably was not known as a righteous woman. She was probably not even known as a righteous woman in God's eyes.

Yesterday we discussed the idea that God allowed Rahab to become part of His family despite her lies to the King. Rahab had lived amid a pagan society in which lying may have been second nature. Her heart prompted her to do what she could to further God's plan and protect His people. To Rahab, that included lying. The focus for Rahab was not the lie itself, but the reason behind it—protection of God's people.

Fortunately, God can be at work in our lives at whatever point we are in our spiritual growth. Just like Rahab, we did not all begin as righteous women. But when we surrender to Him and His plan for our lives, He can start the process of turning us into the women He desires us to become.

The Apostle Paul though requotes Ecclesiastes and reminds us that, in no uncertain terms, not a single one of us is righteous—not even one.

There is no one righteous, not even one (Romans 3:10).

No one is righteous—at least not on our own. But when Jesus gets ahold of us, things change. When we become His, He looks at us through the lens of righteousness.

Although the life of Rahab is recorded in the Book of Joshua, she is mentioned elsewhere throughout Scripture.

In the same way, was not even Rahab the prostitute considered righteous for what she did when she gave lodging to the spies and sent them off in a different direction? (James 2:25)

Rahab was not righteous on her own. She was included with all the rest of us in Romans—all of us *unrighteous ones.* But when Rahab took on the Jewish faith, which included the faith that the Messiah—Jesus—would come one day—then, Rahab too was considered righteous.

Just as Rahab was not righteous until she accepted the one true God, neither are we righteous before we accept Jesus. We were sinners. We deserved eternal judgment. We were not worthy of the grace and mercy and forgiveness Jesus died to give us. But Jesus gave us grace, mercy and forgiveness anyway. And when Jesus forgave our sins, He consecrated us to His purpose and plan. He declared us righteous. He declared us His. That made us holy.

Jesus made us righteous in His eyes. And then He expects us to try to live our lives in a way that reflects how He chooses to see us.

This is Rahab's story. She was not righteous before she took on the one true faith in the one true God. But once she did, she was considered righteous.

When we realize that God has chosen to see us as righteous through His grace, mercy and forgiveness, we understand how God might see His women of faith. We can respond:

I am like Rahab.

For Thought and Discussion

- In what way do you see yourself still as not righteous? In what way do you see yourself as righteous?

- In what way do you think Jesus thinks of you as "holy"? Is that different from being considered righteous?

- How might it be easier for you to understand how God sees you as forgiven?

PRAYER: Dear Jesus, thank you for loving us so much that you choose to see us through the lens of forgiveness. Thank you for loving us even though we are filled with unrighteousness and sin. Thank you for taking all of that away and filling us with your Spirit. Amen.

Day 13— I Will Be Remembered for My Faith

ॐॐ

My Dad's mother was remembered for her fantastic strawberry shortcake. My Mom's Dad was remembered for his snarky sense of humor. It's funny what things we remember about people. When I'm dead and gone, no doubt people will focus on something quirky I do. But hopefully, over and above it all, they will remember that I loved Jesus.

Throughout both the Old and New Testaments, whenever we hear about Rahab, she is referred to as "Rahab the prostitute."

One thousand years after Rahab lived, Paul wrote:

By faith the prostitute Rahab, because she welcomed the spies, was not killed with those who were disobedient (Hebrews 11:31).

Three thousand years after Rahab lived we're still reading about her and learning her lessons. Rahab was famous for helping the Jews take the city of Jericho and thus be able to enter the Promised Land God had given them. She was also famous as being part of the earthly genealogy of Jesus.

Rahab was *infamous* (had a bad reputation) for being a prostitute. All throughout Scripture, whenever Rahab is mentioned, she is referred to as *Rahab the prostitute* (see Joshua 2:1; Joshua 6:22; Joshua 6:25; Hebrews 11:31; James 2:25).

All those verses refer to Rahab and include her profession. They include her reputation. They attach her sin to her name. But something unusual happens when Rahab is personally linked with Jesus. At that point, in the genealogy of Jesus, the focus is no longer on her sin. When she is linked personally with Jesus, it is as if her sin is forgotten and she is listed simply as one of His own. Take a look as Matthew gives the genealogy of Jesus:

> *Salmon the father of Boaz, whose mother was Rahab, Boaz the father of Obed, whose mother was Ruth, Obed the father of Jesse, and Jesse the father of King David* (Matthew 1:5).

Isn't it interesting? When people refer to Rahab, they tack on her shame. But notice—when Rahab is linked to Jesus through His genealogy—God leaves out her shame. It is a concrete, written example of how God focuses not on our past, but on our future with Him.

Brothers and sisters, I do not consider myself yet to have taken hold of it [being like Christ in all things]. But one thing I do: Forgetting what is behind and straining toward what is ahead (Philippians 3:13, explanation added).

Therefore, if anyone is in Christ, the new creation has come: The old has gone, the new is here! (2 Corinthians 5:17).

I, even I, am he who blots out your transgressions, for my own sake, and remembers your sins no more (Isaiah 43:25 and quoted in Hebrews 10:17).

*he does not treat us as our sins deserve or repay us according to our iniquities. For as high as the heavens are above the earth, so great is his love for those who fear him; **as far as the east is from the west, so far has he removed our transgressions from us*** (Psalm 103:10-12, emphasis added).

So often, we struggle to get over our shame; what we did wrong; our sinful past. But God tells us again and again that, once we come to Him, He forgives us and remembers our past no more.

God made us teachable. He wants us to learn from our mistakes. He wants us to turn from our sins and face a new direction—His direction. When He washes us clean of our sins, He gives us a new identity; a new character; a new reputation.

Yes, Rahab had been a prostitute before she turned to the one true God. But once she did, God loved her enough to show her and us that her reputation and who she used to be was no longer what mattered. When she turned to Him, she entered into His family.

People labeled Rahab a prostitute because of what she did. That's not, however, who she was. She was a sinner, saved by grace, redeemed for God's purpose, to be used by Him, taken into His eternal family; loved forever.

Just like you and I are.

Paul highly commends Rahab for her faith and gives her a place on the illustrious roll of the Old Testament of those who triumphed by faith. Look again at our focus Scripture for today:

By faith the prostitute Rahab, because she welcomed the spies, was not killed with those who were disobedient (Hebrews 11:31).

The King James Version says that she Rahab received the spies "with peace." What a sweet touch that is. There was not only faith in her heart that God would be victorious, but also an assured peace when she hid the spies that her deliverance would be taken care of. The implication is that Rahab knew peace from God and peace among mankind because of Him.

The entire Chapter 11 of the Book of Hebrews lists the people of the Old Testament who had great faith. They are referred to as "ancients commended for their faith." They had faith in God, ahead of Jesus, trusting in His promise of salvation to come.

In that list of faithful, Rahab and Sarah are the only two women among the patriarchs of the Old Testament. Along with Abraham, Moses, Noah, David and the other old guys, only Rahab and Sarah represent the women of faith from those days. Ruth isn't mentioned. Neither is Rebecca or Rachael. Not Naomi or Esther. Not even Leah or Hagar are there.

Only Rahab and Sarah are women designated as examples of faith in the great cloud of witnesses. Only God would rank a prostitute along with other saints. Rahab not only had faith, her faith came through in an act of courage. Rahab's inclusion in the Hebrews "cloud of witnesses" points out her life as an example of what all of us are called to do when we take on faith in Jesus.

First, Rahab believed with her heart. She had heard the stories of what the Jewish God had done. She believed them.

Then Rahab confessed with her mouth. She repeated what she had heard about God to the Jewish spies. She confessed her belief that the Jewish God was Lord of heaven and earth.

Then Rahab acted on what she professed to believe. She acted in faith, at the risk of her own life.

God knew Rahab. He knew what her profession was and probably didn't approve of it. But He did approve of her faith. And that was what mattered to Him. Not her past but her future. He wanted her future to be with Him.

This is Rahab's story. She is remembered, not just for her past life, but more importantly, for her faith and for living that faith by taking action.

When we recognize that we will be remembered for our faith and for whether we live that faith, we understand how God might see His women of faith. We can respond:

I am like Rahab.

For Thought and Discussion

- What label do you carry, based on your past? Is this something others gave you or did you label yourself? What new label would you like to wear?

- What label do you think Jesus has ready for you? Ask Him to give you one.

- Rahab believed in her heart; professed with her mouth and then took action to live her faith. In what ways are you doing those things? In what ways might you need to do more?

PRAYER: Dear Jesus, thank you for being the source of our faith and for always proving worthy. Please help us find more ways to profess our faith in you with our mouths and to share your love with others by what we do. Amen.

Day14—I Know the Greater the Sin; the Greater the Love

୬ୡ

Some things I've done in my past make me sigh as I recall my stupidity. Other things make me cringe. Some make me cry and seek out God, thanking Him again for His forgiveness.

I know God has forgiven me the things that only make me sigh and cringe. But I will praise Him forever with all my joyful enthusiasm for the things I've done that make me cry.

It is human nature to think that one sin is worse than another sin to God. It may be. We don't know that for sure though. What we do know is that all sin is disobedience to what God wants for us. All sin hurts our relationship with Him. When we haven't asked for forgiveness, haven't repented, and thus haven't received forgiveness, all our *unforgiven sin* keeps us away from God's love.

In theory, the greater sinner may find it easier to be remorseful and seek forgiveness. Someone who considers herself "a pretty good person," on the other hand, may delay repentance or hope the good outweighs the bad in God's eyes. Unfortunately, one unforgiven sin will keep a person out of heaven; just as one million unforgiven sins will.

It is also human nature by extension to think that if the sin we commit is greater (in our eyes), then the grace we receive is greater. The Apostle Paul struggled to teach the truth surrounding this idea to the church at Rome. He said,

> *What shall we say, then? Shall we go on sinning so that grace may increase? By no means!* (Romans 6:1-2).

Grace is grace. And grace cannot be measured by our human standards. If God has forgiven our sin, He has forgiven all of it. Done deal. He thinks on it no more but has put it as far away from Him as the east is from the west.

> *For as high as the heavens are above the earth, so great is his love for those who fear him; as far as the east is from the west, so far has he removed our transgressions from us* (Psalm 103:11-12).

We, however, keep pulling out our past sins, measuring them with our sin-o-meter and thinking, "wow, that's a whole lot of grace."

Now look at Rahab.

> *In the same way, was not even Rahab the prostitute considered righteous for what she did when she gave lodging to the spies and sent them off in a different direction?* (James 2:25).

Throughout Scripture, Rahab is referred to as "Rahab the prostitute." That is mankind tacking a sin back onto Rahab even though she was considered by God as *righteous;* even though she abandoned her pagan faith and took on the true faith of the one God of the Jews.

From Rahab's human perspective though, maybe she had a strong faith because she had greater experience with sin. Every one of us has a personal testimony of how God has been at work in our lives. But often the most powerful testimonies are from people who once were the biggest sinners. Jesus addresses this in Luke when the woman was weeping and kissing Jesus' feet:

> *"Two people owed money to a certain moneylender. One owed him five hundred denarii, and the other fifty. Neither of them had the money to pay him back, so he forgave the debts of both. Now which of them will love him more?"*
>
> *Simon replied, "I suppose the one who had the bigger debt forgiven."*
>
> *"You have judged correctly," Jesus said.*
>
> *Then he turned toward the woman and said to Simon, "Do you see this woman? I came into your house. You did not give me any water for my feet, but she wet my feet with her tears and wiped them with her hair. You did not give me a kiss, but this woman, from the time I entered, has not stopped kissing my feet. You did not put oil on my head, but she has poured perfume on my feet. Therefore, I tell you, her many sins have been forgiven—as her great love has shown. But **whoever has been forgiven little loves little**"* (Luke 7:41-47, emphasis added).

The woman who anointed Jesus feet with perfume and washed them with her tears was a "sinful woman" but Jesus forgave her and used her life as an example in His parable.

But notice something. Jesus did not say that the woman's sin was greater than someone else's sin and that thus the forgiveness was greater. He said nothing whatsoever about whether God considers one sin greater than another.

Rather, Jesus' point was that *"whoever has been forgiven little loves little."* In other words, Jesus implied that whoever has been forgiven a lot, loves a lot.

When we realize that we sin at all and recognize the depth of Jesus' gift of grace and mercy, all of us can love a lot— regardless of how we personally rank our sin on our human-created sin-o-meter.

Jesus makes the connection that when we realize the depth of our sin and the depth of our forgiveness, something changes *in us*. It's not about how much God has forgiven us in relation to someone else. It's our realization that—wow! God loves me so much! If He can love *me* that much, I can love Him that much. And I can love others that much, too!

It is the understanding of the depth of God's love that makes a person's testimony so powerful.

Jesus also tells us to stop judging other people and their sins because often we can't see clearly because our own sins cloud our eyes (Matthew 7:3-5).

Jesus tells us to leave the judgment up to the Father because when we stand before the throne of Judgment, Jesus will be standing right there next to us, reminding Father God that Jesus already paid the price for us and that our sins have been wiped clean.

It is human nature to judge others and our own sins. It is God's nature to grant us grace and mercy through Jesus' sacrifice.

This is Rahab's story. She had lived a sinful life, but because she turned to the one true God, she—and others—knew He had made her righteous.

When we realize the depth of God's love for us that He forgave our sins, we increase our love for Him and for others and understand how He might see His women of faith. We can respond:

I am like Rahab.

For Thought and Discussion

- What, in your view, is the greatest sin a person could commit? Why do you feel it is greater than another?

- Scripture tells us that the only unforgivable sin is blaspheme against the Holy Spirit (Matthew 12:31)—stubbornly not asking for forgiveness when the Spirit prompts us to. Are there areas of your life where you clearly sense the Spirit prompting you to ask for forgiveness?

- Are you withholding love or forgiveness from someone because you feel their sin is greater than your own? How might God see the situation? How should you see it?

PRAYER: Dear Jesus, thank you so much for your forgiveness. Thank you for your mercy so that we don't receive what we deserve. Thank you for your grace so that we do receive what we don't deserve. Please help us remember that all sin is disobedience to you, no matter how great or small. Help us take the love we feel from your forgiveness and return it to you and extend it to others. Amen.

I Can Be Used by God

Day 15—God Can Use Anyone

తిళ్ళి

When my faith was young, it never occurred to me that God might want to use me to accomplish something big. I figured there were others He had set aside for that purpose—preachers, scholars, missionaries. Who was I? What did I know about doctrine and theology? I was just little me.

It has been a long journey to understanding that God wants to use me for His purpose and that He has even trained me up for that purpose—or at least can provide me with the skills, understanding, time, people or tools I need to get the job done. My writing of inspirational pieces, meditations, devotionals and these character studies are proof that God has been using me for a purpose I certainly never set out to accomplish.

Even though I don't hold a degree from a theological seminary.

Jericho was a large city. In the city were shopkeepers, farmers, potters, priests and teachers. Even the King of Jericho lived there. Many of the people who lived there were possibly even "good people"—people who tried to live with kindness towards their neighbor. But it was Rahab—the prostitute—that God sought out and used for His purpose.

So often, God passes over the rich and famous and seeks out the lowly, the unknown, the outcast people in society to bless and bring into His plan. Moses was on the run, having murdered an Egyptian. He was also humble and without confidence in his ability to lead God's people. The shepherds, one of the lowest groups of Jewish society, were the first people to whom the Messiah's birth was announced by the angels. Jesus' disciple Matthew was a hated tax collector. Peter, James and John were fishermen. All these people were lowly or outcast members of society who were used to further God's plan.

James and Paul talk a lot about the difference between faith and works. We know that we are saved by grace and mercy—given freely to us by Jesus through His sacrifice. There is nothing we can do on our own to earn our way to heaven.

But James also reminds us that once we have been saved; once we realize how much we owe to Jesus for His forgiveness, we want to express our faith and our love for Him by what we do. James reminds us of this by referring back to Rahab.

> *You see that a person is considered righteous by what they do and not by faith alone. In the same way, was not even Rahab the prostitute considered righteous for what she did when she gave lodging to the spies and sent them off in a different direction?* (James 2:24-25).

God saved Rahab because she believed. She only had a brand-new faith, but it was enough that she was saved spiritually and physically. Because of that faith, she also did what she knew she had to do. She did what would help God accomplish His plan for His people. She allowed God to use her for that purpose.

Jesus' mother Mary also had faith. And then Mary willingly let God use her for His purpose. Not knowing *how* God would accomplish what the angel told her would happen, Mary said:

"I am the Lord's servant," Mary answered. "May your word to me be fulfilled." Then the angel left her (Luke 1:38).

The Apostle Paul had more to say about living our faith by taking action for God.

For it is by grace you have been saved, through faith—and this is not from yourselves, it is the gift of God—not by works, so that no one can boast. For we are God's handiwork, created in Christ Jesus **to do good works, which God prepared in advance for us to do** (Ephesians 2:8-10, emphasis added).

There is a connection between faith and action. We are saved by our faith in God's grace when we ask and receive His forgiveness through Jesus. Once saved, then our love for God urges us to allow God to use us for His purpose.

This is Rahab's story. She had faith in the one true God. It was her faith that saved her, but because she had faith, she willingly risked her life in order to be of use to God in accomplishing His plan.

When we realize the depth of what Jesus did for us on the cross and seek to show our love for Him by happily allowing God to use us for His purpose, we understand how God might see His women of faith. We can respond:

I am like Rahab.

For Thought and Discussion

- Do you sometimes think you can win God's favor by doing things for Him? How can you get over that idea?

- Do you recognize that a desire to work for God comes from your love for Him and gratitude for his grace and mercy? When did you first discover this and cross the line from duty to desire to serve?

- Do you sense God leading you to do something for His kingdom? Do you feel incapable or unsuited? How can you jump into the work joyfully and with more confidence?

PRAYER: Dear Jesus, we can't quite get our minds around the depth of what you have done for us. But knowing how much you love us makes us want to return that love by being your hands and feet in this world. Please help us see what you are doing around us and show us how we can help. Amen.

Day 16—I See God's Power

Each New Year, I settle on one or two writing projects I would like to accomplish over the year. Then I pray over the goals and set off happily working to achieve them. But this year, something different happened.

I determined two books I wanted to work on. For several days afterwards, I felt unsettled. I tried to work on the two books, but was less than productive. So I prayed. After I asked God to lead my writing for the year, He instantly placed a question in my heart:

Why are you trying to limit what I can do through you?

Me trying to limit God? I then asked Him to direct my writing to where He wanted me to go. He responded the same hour with eight book titles He wanted me to work on that year. Not complete and see published—but work on. By the end of the year I had written and published five of those books and had the others fleshed out enough to understand their direction. God was proving His power to me in a personal way since I couldn't have written those books within a year without the leading and strength God provided.

This experience reminded me of what Jesus said to His disciples about the difficulty of entering the kingdom of heaven.

Jesus looked at them and said, "With man this is impossible, but with God all things are possible" (Matthew 19:26).

Imagine Rahab watching the Israelites gather just outside the city. With the men, women and children, the Israelites numbered millions. But it was not the vastness of the Jewish numbers that gave Rahab faith. It was the stories of God's power that convinced Rahab to join His team.

We have heard how the Lord dried up the water of the Red Sea for you when you came out of Egypt, and what you did to Sihon and Og, the two kings of the Amorites east of the Jordan, whom you completely destroyed. When we heard of it, our hearts melted in fear and everyone's courage failed because of you, for the Lord your God is God in heaven above and on the earth below (Joshua 2:10-11).

Scripture records how God showed people His power. Rahab's reaction was to join His team. Rahab had probably lived her whole life within the walls of Jericho. She and everyone she knew no doubt felt those walls protected her. But she had heard about God's power. When she compared God's power to the strength of Jericho's walls, she knew His power was greater.

God created the entire universe. He can do anything He sets His mind to. And sometimes He likes to prove His power. For example God sent Gideon to fight the Midianites. But before the battle, God told Gideon he had too many men, saying that if God won the battle, Israel would boast about their own strength. So first God reduced Gideon's army from 22,000 men to 10,000.

Then God reduced it to 300. (Judges 7) God won the battle in a way that proved His power beyond any doubt.

Similarly, scrawny teenage David faced the giant Goliath—armed with a sling and a pebble and wearing—not King Saul's armor, but the armor of God

> *"All those gathered here will know that it is not by sword or spear that the Lord saves; for the battle is the Lord's, and he will give all of you into our hands"* *(1 Samuel 17:47).*

David fought and slew the giant but recognized that it was God who did it, through him, proving to everyone the enormity of God's power.

Seeing the power of God is also Rahab's story. She had heard about God's power. Based on hearing, she chose to believe. Ultimately, she saw that power herself.

When we recognize God's power and see it in our own lives and in the lives of others, we understand how God might see His women of faith. We can respond:

I am like Rahab.

For Thought and Discussion

- What in nature best shows you God's power? What about it proves power?

- Was there an event in your life or in someone else's life that proved God's power in a way that could not be explained away? How did that effect your faith?

- Is there any way you might be trying to limit what God can do in your life or through your efforts? How might you break free and allow Him control of the situation?

PRAYER: Dear Jesus, thank you for proving your power. We worship you, Father for who you are and recognize that you have power and authority over all the earth. Holy Spirit, we want to give you more power in our own lives. Please help us attune our thoughts and actions to your leading. Amen.

Day 17—I Help Others on God's Team

It's time for you to giggle at how silly I am. At age 64, I finally confess that I never chose a favorite color, because—wait for it—I was worried that all the other colors would feel bad.

No, I don't really believe colors have feelings. The point is that sometimes it's hard to make choices. In some deep recess of my brain I must have felt that if I chose a favorite color, I didn't have the opportunity to like the other colors just as much. It was as if once I made a choice, I was stuck with it.

Now, if you ask me, I'll tell you that my favorite color is "rainbow." Gotcha!

Rahab chose sides in the battle around her. She knew whose side would be the winning side. Yes, she made a deal to save her family, but she recognized God's power and chose to join His team.

Then Rahab did something about it. She didn't just join His team, she stepped out in faith, put on her big-girl boots and placed her very life in jeopardy for what she believed. She lied to her king and enabled the Jewish spies to escape. If she had been found out, we might now celebrate the life of Rahab as a martyr rather than as a woman in Jesus' lineage. Or we would have forgotten about her entirely.

Our Christian heritage is filled with people who were killed for their faith. No one hopes to join that list of faithful. But all of us should hope to be on the list of believers who live for their faith.

Sometimes there is strife within a local church. It is painful to experience. No doubt it grieves Jesus when He sees His children not playing nicely together. But even when a church is getting along, there is always room for ways we can help each other. There are ministries we can participate in. There are people to visit and encouragement to give.

> *...Joshua spared Rahab the prostitute, with her family and all who belonged to her, because she hid the men Joshua had sent as spies to Jericho—**and she lives among the Israelites to this day*** (Joshua 6:25, emphasis added).

That verse makes you wonder what Rahab did to help others on God's team once she began living among the Israelites. Jewish law would have forbidden her from pursuing her former profession. And no doubt, her new faith in God would have changed her heart to no longer pursue that profession. But perhaps, she continued to exhibit her ability to welcome people and make them feel at ease.

> *By faith the prostitute Rahab, because **she welcomed the spies**, was not killed with those who were disobedient* (Hebrews 11:31, emphasis added).

We know from Scripture that Rahab was declared righteous. She also married a godly Jewish man and became the mother of Boaz. Boaz was the man whom Ruth the widow married. Boaz was known as a man of character, often compared in his character and actions to Jesus. It was Rahab who raised Boaz to be that man of high character and he later was included, along with Rahab in the named genealogy of Jesus.

Rahab's example can make us consider what we might do today to help members of God's team. Here are a few verses to remind us of this duty.

> *And do not forget to do good and to share with others, for with such sacrifices God is pleased* (Hebrews 13:16).

> *If anyone has material possessions and sees a brother or sister in need but has no pity on them, how can the love of God be in that person?* (1 John 3:17).

> *Carry each other's burdens, and in this way you will fulfill the law of Christ* (Galatians 6:2)

> *Therefore encourage one another and build each other up, just as in fact you are doing* (1 Thessalonians 5:11).

This is Rahab's story. She joined God's team and then set about doing what she could to help them do their part in accomplishing God's plan.

When we realize that God desires us to help other people who love Him and when we do so, we understand how God might see His women of faith. We can respond:

I am like Rahab.

For Thought and Discussion

- Is there a need in my church or the world at large that no one is fulfilling? How can I go about filling it?

- Is there a ministry—within my local church or outside of it—that God is calling me to participate in?

- How can I personally help others on God's team?

PRAYER: Dear Father God, thank you for adopting us into your family. Thank you for your church and for the many people who love you. Please open my eyes to where I can fill a need and be a help and encouragement to other members of your team. Amen.

Day 18—I Know God Sees Me

❧

When my husband and I would move to a new town, one of the things we would do was look for a church home. Sometimes, that meant we would attend several different churches before finding one that clicked with our personality and worship styles. As a general rule, we felt conspicuous when we attended a smaller church. Folks would approach us and welcome us and invite us to the next few events, sometimes following up with a phone call or visit. When we visited a large church, however, we felt inconspicuous and safe. God, however, still saw us, wherever we were.

Sometimes we focus on Rahab's circumstances within the city of Jericho. We sing the song and read the words about how God made those hugely fortified walls of Jericho "come tumbling down." God's army completely destroyed the city of Jericho and everyone in it—everyone except for Rahab and her family.

> *Joshua said to the two men who had spied out the land, "**Go into the prostitute's house** and bring her out and all who belong to her, in accordance with your oath to her." So the young men who had done*

the spying went in and brought out Rahab, her father and mother, her brothers and sisters and all who belonged to her. They brought out her entire family and put them in a place outside the camp of Israel (Joshua 6:22-23, emphasis added).

Did you notice? After the Jewish army blew the trumpets and shouted; after the walls fell; after the city was defeated, *then* the spies went into Rahab's house to rescue her. That house, you remember was built into a portion of the city wall. Imagine the scene. The formidable city wall; 14 feet wide or wider and probably several stories tall was completely in ruin, all except for the one portion of the wall containing Rahab's home—the scarlet cord still flying in the breeze from her window.

How carefully God had orchestrated the battle. Not only did the walls fall through the supernatural power of praise created by the Jewish army playing trumpets and shouting. But God accomplished it all with surgical precision; leaving one section intact and protecting the home's inhabitants as promised by God's representatives—the Jewish spies.

Scripture says that after Rahab and her family were rescued, then the Jewish army burned the whole city and everything in it. Jericho was totally destroyed. At that point, perhaps Rahab's home and the part of the wall in which it was built, collapsed also. Or perhaps it further crumbled over time. Regardless of the timing, we know that God caused the wall to fall, but preserved the portion that protected Rahab and her family.

God was aware of Rahab and saved her.

One further point about Rahab's home. In Rahab's circumstances in a pagan society that did not have the same moral code that God's people had, there may not have been a social stigma for her profession among her own people. She may have been a wealthy woman because of her profession. She might have been well known in her society, perhaps even known as a businesswoman.

We don't know everything about the culture and her position in it, but we do know that her home was right there in a focal position in the city. Not only was it a good location for her specific business, it was also an ideal location for the spies to be able to scout the city and get a perspective both as to what was happening and where inside the city as well as a perspective from the wall, looking outside, where the Jewish army would be.

In other words, regardless of Rahab's profession and whether she was considered a woman of ill repute in her own society, God had placed her in exactly the right location to be able to be used by Him—via the scouting spies. She was also in exactly the right location to be able to be saved from destruction where the spies could locate her easily and bring her out of the city before it was completely destroyed.

God not only placed her in the location best suited to further His plan; He also placed her where she would be safe during the battle, enabling the spies to rescue her later.

God noticed her.

This is Rahab's story. Her home was located in exactly the right place so that she and her family could be saved. God made sure the battle did not destroy her before He could assure her rescue.

When we realize that God often places us exactly where He wants us and when we know without doubt that He is aware of us, we understand how God might see His women of faith. We can respond:

I am like Rahab.

For Thought and Discussion

- Picture the "battle" for Jericho—the Jewish army marching around the city, priests blowing trumpets and then heading back to camp for the evening; to return the next day and do it again. Imagine the people inside watching, maybe even laughing. Imagine when the wall fell, how Rahab must have felt knowing her home on one section of the wall was still standing. How might experiencing those events have strengthened her faith? How might Rahab's story strengthen your faith today?

- If Rahab's profession was not considered immoral by her society, how hard would it have been to leave it behind for an unknown future with only fledgling faith? Under what circumstances would you leave everything?

- Has there been an experience in your life when you knew for certain God was aware of your circumstances? Or where He saved you from ruin? Explain.

PRAYER: Heavenly Father, you are aware of us every second of every day. Thank you for always keeping an eye on us. Thank you especially for saving us from utter destruction and ruin when everything around us is threatened. Amen.

I Witness

Day 19—I Know the Power of Evangelism

As a Christian who trusts God, I wonder how anyone could ever choose not to be on God's side. God is all powerful. He knows all things. His plan is perfect. He only wants what is good for us and for His world. And Scripture tells us in the Book of Revelation, that God wins the battle against evil.

Why would a person *not* believe and be saved?

Recently, God has been nudging me to evangelize, placing Matthew 28:16-20 on my heart.

> *Then the eleven disciples went to Galilee, to the mountain where Jesus had told them to go. When they saw him, they worshiped him; but some doubted. Then Jesus came to them and said, "All authority in heaven and on earth has been given to me. Therefore go and make disciples of all nations, baptizing them in the name of the Father and of the Son and of the Holy Spirit, and teaching them to obey everything I have commanded you. And surely I am with you always, to the very end of the age"* (Matthew 28:16-20).

Yes, Jesus gave that "great commission" to His eleven living disciples, just before He returned to heaven. But as modern followers of Jesus, we also are His disciples. Therefore, by proxy, Jesus has commanded us also to go and tell the world about Him. And isn't it interesting that at the same time Jesus told his disciples (and us) to tell others about Him, He also assured us He would always be with us?

Sometimes we hesitate to evangelize. Society warns us not to make other people uncomfortable. We feel unworthy of introducing Jesus to others. We feel incapable—not understanding theology or Scripture enough to be able to answer questions or lead people to acceptance.

All of that is us being insecure. It's up to us to seek the strength and guidance of the Holy Spirit. It's up to us to get over our insecurity, simply introduce Jesus to other people and let Him take it from there.

Rahab had heard the stories of how God had delivered his people from slavery and how He had brought them through the Red Sea and beyond the wilderness. She knew His power and she knew that the right side to be on in the coming battle was God's side.

We too know how God has delivered us from our slavery to sin. We know how God has brought us through flood and desert. We know His power and we too want to be on God's side in the ongoing spiritual battle and the coming battle.

Rahab had heard the stories about the Jewish people's victory—God's victory. She may not have had a Jewish evangelist knock on her door and hand her a copy of the Book of Moses. But she had heard. Someone in her life had told her. The stories might have been told as gossip ("Did you hear?") Or maybe she had heard it from a person who knew the Jewish God personally and lived his life in faith.

After the battle of Jericho, Rahab went to live with the Jewish people. No doubt, her new family and friends *did* profess their faith to her personally. No doubt, their testimony *did* strengthen her own faith. No doubt the Jewish people began the process of discipleship—explaining their faith and how to live it.

At some point God had given Rahab intuition or discernment to know that the spies were men of God, the forerunners of His people who were to carry out His will. God somehow revealed to her that to take sides with the Jewish spies was to take sides with God Himself.

Further, there was in Rahab's mind, a call from God. God had singled Rahab out from all of the people in her town to help Him. That call made her willing to sacrifice her own people—an act of treason, punishable by her death. Declaring her faith in God, Rahab earned a unique place among the women whose lives are recorded in Scripture. She chose to be on God's side, regardless of the consequences to her.

This is Rahab's story. She recognized the power of God and chose Him when He called to her. She chose God over everything she knew, what others believed and even over her own society. She then stepped out in faith.

When we recognize that God calls to us and that part of His call is to then go out into the world and share His plan through Jesus with others, we understand how God might see His women of faith. We can respond:

I am like Rahab.

For Thought and Discussion

- Do you think Rahab heard mere gossip about God or do you think she heard directly from Jewish people who had faith? Which would have been more impactful?

- Where did you first hear about Jesus? In what ways do you tell others about Jesus? What could you do differently, or in addition to, or more of? Will you?

- How do you work to disciple other Christians? How have you been discipled?

PRAYER: Dear Jesus, thank you for giving us the ability and the opportunity to choose you. Thank you for also first having chosen us—by making it possible at all to become your children by what you did on the cross. Please give us words and encouragement to tell others about you and your love for them. Amen.

Day 20—I Have a Scarlet Cord

❧

When my husband and I visited Amsterdam, one of our evening meanderings took us to the "red light" district. No, we shouldn't have been there and we left quickly. But what we noticed was that there were indeed red light bulbs in the light fixtures.

When I think of Rahab the prostitute hanging the scarlet cord outside her window, it reminds me of the "red light" district in Amsterdam and the big red "A" Hester Prynne wore in Nathanial Hawthorne's novel *The Scarlet Letter.* In both the story of Rahab and Hester Prynne, the color red could represent both sin as well as salvation.

When the Israelites were preparing to leave Egypt, God sent plagues to convince Pharaoh to let His people go. Most of those plagues affected the Jewish people also. Those flies, gnats, bloody water and other horrible plagues had to also be endured by the Jewish people. But God specifically wanted to save His people from the time the angel of death went through the land of Egypt, killing all of the first born children.

In order to protect the Jewish people, God instructed them to sacrifice a lamb and smear the blood of that lamb over the doorframe of their homes. When the angel of the Lord came through the land of Egypt to kill the firstborn, he would "pass over" those homes with the bloody signal indicating the home containing God's people.

> *"The blood will be a sign for you on the houses where you are, and when I see the blood, I will pass over you"* (Exodus 12:13).

Many Bible scholars are quick to point out the symbolic similarity between the red cord hung over Rahab's window and the blood of the sacrificial lamb the Israelites smeared over the door frames in Egypt. In Egypt, the blood of the lamb signaled the angel of death to pass over those homes. The red blood meant earthly salvation for the people inside.

For Rahab, the scarlet cord hanging outside her window signaled the Israelites to pass over her home during the battle. That blood red cord meant earthly salvation for Rahab and her family inside.

> *So she sent them* (the spies) *away, and they departed. And she tied the scarlet cord in the window* (Joshua 2:21, explanation added).

When Jesus died, red came to symbolize His blood that was shed so we who believe in Him have eternal salvation. The shedding of His blood symbolically and spiritually marked us as His. Thus, marked and sealed, we belong to Him and our souls are now secure from eternal death. Symbolically, we Christians have a blood red cord that signals our salvation. We are to hang it over our windows, our doorframes and our hearts, reminding us and others that we have been spiritually saved by the blood of the Lamb of God.

This is Rahab's story. She had a scarlet cord. She knew the cord meant safety for herself and her family. God knew about her newfound faith. The cord was not exhibited as proof to Him; but as visual evidence to the Jews of her faith and expected salvation.

When we realize that Jesus' sacrifice is symbolically like Rahab's scarlet cord and provides for our eternal safety, we understand how God might see His women of faith. We can respond:

I am like Rahab.

For Thought and Discussion

- What thoughts do you have about how sin and salvation are resolved through the blood of Jesus?

- What new thoughts do you have about the symbolic relationship between the Passover blood and Rahab's scarlet cord?

- Which do you think red represents better: sin or salvation? Why?

PRAYER: Dear Jesus, thank you for your blood sacrifice. Thank you for stories in Scripture of people who recognize you as savior and forgiver of sin. Thank you for providing us with a symbolic scarlet cord that reminds us of your salvation. Amen.

Day 21—I Display My Scarlet Cord

Every national holiday or patriotic occasion, my husband gets the flag out and hangs it on our porch. It's a symbol for everyone to see—that our household is proud to live in America.

Yesterday we discussed how Rahab's scarlet cord represented her salvation from the Jewish army bent on destroying the city of Jericho. In order to secure her safety, Rahab was required to display that scarlet cord in her window so the Jewish army could see it.

Although the reason behind Rahab's scarlet cord may not have been understood by the other people in Jericho, nonetheless, it was a symbol to the world that she had placed her faith in God's army. By displaying it, she was telling the Jewish people and the rest of the world about her faith.

Rahab's scarlet cord hung out her window while she waited for deliverance. Just like Rahab, all we have to do is take Jesus into our hearts and wait for Him to deliver us. We've done our part in making the decision and acting upon it. Now we wait for His deliverance. Jesus, in fact, has already done His part—on the cross when He provided the blood sacrifice that wiped out our sins forever.

What this day's lesson stresses is that while we're waiting for Jesus to return for us, it's up to us to keep our scarlet cord hanging out there for the world to see. Yes, the spies placed the cord in Rahab's window to mark her house when the Jews returned. But we can expand the significance for our lives in application of this lesson.

Having Jesus' salvation is wonderful. But we have a duty to more than just own His salvation for ourselves. We should hang our scarlet cord on our homes. We should wear our scarlet cord each day. We should share our scarlet cord with others. And we should help other people hang a scarlet cord out their own windows.

When we take hold of Jesus' scarlet cord of salvation, it should be visible to the world. Our homes and our lives should be an evident representation of Christ's love for us and for others.

This is Rahab's story. She displayed the scarlet cord. Not only did she know it was there, the Jewish army knew it was there, too as did everyone in the city of Jericho and outside of it.

When we realize that Jesus wants us to display our faith in Him to the world and share Him with others, we understand how God might see His women of faith. We can respond:

I am like Rahab.

For Thought and Discussion

- Do you wear a cross necklace, have a fish sticker on your car or display another symbol of Christianity? Do you use those symbols as a reason to introduce others to Jesus?

- In what way can you use the image of Rahab's scarlet rope to remember Jesus' desire that we display our salvation and share it with others?

- What other symbols of Jesus or your faith might you display to share with others?

PRAYER: Dear Jesus, thank you for giving us minds and hearts that can be reminded of you through objects we see. Please help us to use items in our everyday lives as ways to open conversations about you. Amen.

Day 22—I Work to Save My Family

❧✺

Recently I was fleshing out the chapters of a book I wanted to write about worry. To gather information, I posted a question on Facebook, asking what people's top two or three sources of worry were. The number one answer from my Christian friends was that they worried over their family's salvation.

Wouldn't it be great if we could bring everyone we knew with us to heaven just because we want them to believe? Unfortunately, there's no way we can save anyone. All we can do is introduce people to Jesus and let Him work on their hearts and minds until they one day choose to give control of their lives to Him.

When we meet Rahab, she is living in a home built within one of the walls of Jericho. She had a home business, you might say, as a prostitute. We don't know if any of her family members lived there with her. It's possible she was shunned by family members because of her profession. More likely, given the immoral society in which she lived, she was not considered any more immoral than anyone else.

But she loved her family, just like we love our family today. Imagine what Rahab must have thought. She looked out her window and saw the millions of people camped across the river. She knew the Jewish army intended to attack her city. She had heard about the power of the Jewish God. She recognized the very real threat they were to her safety and the safety of her family. She was desperate to save them. So she made her hopeful, but urgent demand of the Jewish spies.

> "Now then, please swear to me by the Lord that you will show kindness to my family, because I have shown kindness to you. Give me a sure sign that you will spare the lives of my father and mother, my brothers and sisters, and all who belong to them— and that you will save us from death" (Joshua 2: 11-13).

Rahab was concerned not only for herself but for her family also. She could have made a deal with the Jewish spies to simply save herself. But her deal was that the Jewish army would not only save her but her family as well.

Basically, Rahab worked to bring her family with her into the family of God. In fact, God wants us to bring all of our family members into His house, too.

> But as for me and my household, we will serve the Lord" (Joshua 24:15).

> Start children off on the way they should go, and even when they are old they will not turn from it (Proverbs 22:6).

Although we can't force anyone to accept Jesus' salvation, we can tell them about Him. We can let His light shine through us. We can live a life that honors Him. We can share with them what knowing Jesus has meant to us and how He has changed our lives.

This is Rahab's story. She fought for the salvation of her family. Then she brought them into God's family with her.

When we realize the importance of sharing Jesus with others in our lives and when we do so enthusiastically, we understand how God might see His women of faith. We can respond:

I am like Rahab.

For Thought and Discussion

- Was there someone in your family who introduced you to Jesus or shared His love with you? If not, how might that have encouraged you?

- Is there someone in your family who does not yet know Jesus? Have you introduced Him to them? What might you do to encourage their faith?

- Is there someone in your family who knows Jesus because you helped them know Him? How might that experience encourage you to share Jesus with others?

PRAYER: Dear Jesus, thank you for loving us. Thank you for loving others also. Please guide us when we try to share your love with people who don't know you. Please remind us that the saving is up to you but encourage us not to stop telling others about you. Amen.

My Future

Day 23—I Joined God's People

When I was a kid I thought Christ was Jesus' last name. To the people who knew Jesus, He was probably referred to as Jesus, son of Joseph. When people who knew who Jesus was referred to Him, it was Jesus *the Christ*. In Greek, the word *Christ* means "anointed." In Hebrew culture, prophets, priests and kings were anointed with oil, in a ceremony. Pouring holy oil on the head of a person set that person apart for a special task for God.

Referring to Jesus the Christ, basically points to the fact that King Jesus was anointed by God for the task of salvation.

Throughout the Old Testament, we see the history of the Jewish people—the descendants of Abraham—referred to again and again as God's "chosen people." As God's chosen people, He protected them. He led them. He provided for them. And He loved them, even when they ignored Him, disobeyed Him or turned away from Him.

> *For you are a people holy to the Lord your God. The Lord your God has chosen you out of all the peoples on the face of the earth to be his people, his treasured possession* (Deuteronomy 7:6).

Blessed is the nation whose God is the Lord, the people he chose for his inheritance (Psalm 33:12).

When Rahab was saved by the Jewish spies, she and her family left Jericho and lived among the Jewish people. She became part of their nation. Her faith in their God brought her into the family of His chosen people.

Enter Jesus. Our New Testament section of the Holy Bible is filled with the truth of the fulfillment of Old Testament prophecy through Jesus. God told His chosen people He would send a Messiah to save them. He sent Jesus. God told His chosen people that He would prove His everlasting love for them. Jesus died for them.

The best part of that plan is that Jesus came to save us, too. Even though we may not be part of the Jewish people, Jesus came to prove His everlasting love for us, too.

When we recognize the truth in that and take hold of what Jesus did for us, we are adopted into God's family. Until then, all of us people in the world are God's *creations* and He loves us. But when we seek to belong to Jesus' family, God the Father adopts us and we join His family. We become His *children*.

We become part of God's chosen people.

As Jesus said, "I chose you before the creation of the world" (John 15:16; Ephesians 1:4).

If you belong to Christ, then you are Abraham's seed, and heirs according to the promise (Galatians 3:29).

Abraham was the father of all the Jewish people. It is through His lineage that all Jewish people come. It was with Abraham that God made his first covenant, promising them to be His chosen people if they remained faithful to Him.

This verse tells us that when we come to Jesus and accept Him into our hearts, giving over our lives to Him, we become part of His eternal family; His chosen people, just as if we were descendants of Abraham himself.

Rahab became part of God's people, too. She turned away from her pagan society and her life in it. She turned to the one true God. She became part of the Jewish community, marrying into it and bearing Jewish children so that ultimately she also became biologically part of the Jewish nation through her children. She joined God's people.

> *So the young men who had done the spying went in and brought out Rahab, her father and mother, her brothers and sisters and all who belonged to her. They brought out her entire family and put them in a place outside the camp of Israel* (Joshua 6:23).

The spies brought out Rahab's entire family from the rubble of Jericho. They did so after the majority of the wall fell and before the rest of the army completely destroyed every living thing inside the city.

But notice. They didn't just let Rahab and her family go off on their own to meander the countryside. They took her entire family to a place outside the camp of Israel. The laws of Moses had specific rules for making sure that the people were kept safe from health issues. The Book of Leviticus goes on *ad nausea* about the rules and regulations dealing with touching unclean objects and how a person must go about being purified before being let back into the rest of the community.

It would have been normal and expected, not to say required by the Jewish laws, to have kept Rahab and her family outside the camp while the army was finishing up the battle for Jericho. Once that task was completed, or perhaps while it was being finished, Rahab and her family could be assessed for health issues, perhaps they were prayed over. Surely they were comforted and gratitude expressed over Rahab's part in God's battle. No doubt Rahab herself expressed gratitude, perhaps even praying along with the Jewish people around her.

But even after Rahab and her family had been attended to, they were not abandoned by the Jewish people. Rahab and her family could have left the Jews behind and headed to a neighboring town to start over. No doubt, Rahab's fledgling faith was beginning to blossom, having seen the destruction of her indestructible city by means that could only have been seen as supernatural. No doubt, Rahab recognized the honor of the Jewish people in following through on their promise to save her and her family. She likely wanted to be part of a people who honored their word.

The Jewish people accepted Rahab and her family as one of them and Rahab joined the community willingly.

> *But Joshua spared Rahab the prostitute, with her family and all who belonged to her, because she hid the men Joshua had sent as spies to Jericho—and she lives among the Israelites to this day* (Joshua 6:25).

Rahab lived among the Israelites "to this day," whenever that day was that the words were written. And evidently Rahab remained a part of the community of Israelites, even married into it and joined the lineage of Jesus.

This is Rahab's story. She chose to adopt faith in the one true God. As a result, she was brought into the family of God's chosen people.

When we realize that God adopts us into His family and that in fact, He chose us before we were ever born, we understand how God might see His women of faith. We can respond:

I am like Rahab.

For Thought and Discussion

- How does knowing you are in God's family make you feel about carrying on the family name—Christian?

- How does being part of God's family give you special love or allowance for other Christians? Or does it make you feel like we have a higher standard to live up to?

- What does being part of God's inheritance mean to you?

PRAYER: Dear Jesus, thank you for family. Thank you for adopting us into your family. Please remind us that even though we can't choose our earthly family members, we are so grateful that you have chosen us to be part of your family forever. Amen.

Day 24—I See Grace Amid Justice

Once in third grade I was listening to my dad preach a sermon. What I remember most was that I didn't have a clue what Dad was talking about. Dad's message was about God giving us grace. All I knew about grace was that it was what *we* said to God, just before we stuffed our faces with food. Surely Dad wasn't implying that God said grace to me before sitting down to eat His lunch. The scope of my language has improved considerably over the years.

Now I understand the meaning of grace. Grace is receiving what we don't deserve. Grace is the opposite of mercy, which is *not* getting what we *do* deserve. Fortunately, God gives us both grace and mercy in abundance. God gives us grace—what we don't deserve: salvation, forgiveness, eternity in His presence. God *doesn't* give us what we do deserve: hellfire and damnation. That's mercy.

As for what we say before meals, saying grace is our chance to express our gratitude for God's provision—even though we don't deserve it. *Saying grace* is verbally (even if silently) acknowledging the grace God gives.

Along with grace, God grants favor to those who love Him. Favor is preferential treatment. At the minimum, that preferential treatment includes spiritual protection throughout our earthly lives. It also includes spiritual protection with Him in heaven forever, free from evil and harm. Here are a few verses that talk about how God favors His people:

Surely, Lord, you bless the righteous; you surround them with your favor as with a shield (Psalm 5:23).

May the favor of the Lord our God rest on us; establish the work of our hands for us—yes, establish the work of our hands (Psalm 90:17).

For the Lord God is a sun and shield; the Lord bestows favor and honor; no good thing does he withhold from those whose walk is blameless (Psalm 84:11).

Rahab would have heard the stories; she knew who the Jews were and who their God was. Then she trusted and believed. Imagine what it might have been like for Rahab. As a prostitute, she might have been scorned by the people of Jericho. But she would have known people. She might have had friendships with other women in town; perhaps she had family members who did not make it to the safety of her home to be spared.

Rahab had been spared God's judgment because of her new faith. But she would have been painfully aware that the rest of her town had not been spared. There would have been no doubt for Rahab that her faith in God had proved that He granted her His favor, and granted her grace—sparing her life, even though she didn't deserve it.

Often we modern folk, knowing the loving kindness preached by Jesus, wonder how the God of the Old Testament could have slaughtered so many people. But the God of the Old

Testament is the same God as the God of the New Testament. God had made a covenant not only with the Jews but also with the Gentiles, when He told Ishmael (Abraham's first son by the servant Hagar) that God would make Ishmael's descendants into a great nation. In fact, Ishmael's descendants became the Gentile people who settled in Canaan, many of whom ethnically became the Arab people. God had told the Jews that it would take four hundred years for Ishmael's descendants to completely abandon God.

> *Then the Lord said to him* [Abraham], *"Know for certain that for four hundred years your descendants will be strangers in a country not their own* [Egypt] *and that they will be enslaved and mistreated there. But I will punish the nation they serve as slaves, and afterward they will come out with great possessions"* (Genesis 15:13-14, explanation added).

God also specifically made a covenant with Ishmael's offspring, giving them the Promised Land *if* they remained faithful to Him.

> *"And I will give to you* [Abraham] *and to your offspring* [including Ishmael] *after you the land of your sojournings, all the land of Canaan, for an everlasting possession, and I will be their God."* (Genesis 17:8, explanation added)

The covenant above that included Ishmael—as part Abraham's offspring, was given to Abraham before Abraham's other son Isaac (whose offspring became the Jewish nation) was even born.

> *Then Abraham took Ishmael his son and all those born in his house or bought with his money, every*

male among the men of Abraham's house, and he circumcised the flesh of their foreskins that very day, as God had said to him—partook in the human male part of the covenant by being circumcised along with the other male members of Abraham's family (Genesis 17:23).

The covenant with God was simple: God's part was to give Abraham's offspring the land of Canaan and to be their God. Abraham's family part was *to be faithful to God.*

Unfortunately, those Gentiles who descended through Ishmael did not keep their part of covenant to remain faithful. Therefore, our just God planned to cleanse the land of the unfaithful who by then were worshiping idols and give that land to the other part of Abraham's line (the Jews through Isaac) who *had* kept the covenant. In Rahab's time, some of those unfaithful people descending from Ishmael then lived in Canaan.

This covenant breaking by Ishmael's line and the covenant keeping by Isaac's line is why Joshua and the army set out to destroy Jericho so they could take the land of Canaan as promised by God. Jericho was a great big settlement filled with people descended from Ishmael who had not kept the covenant. When God planned to destroy the city, he was operating from a point of justice. There were consequences to the people of Canaan who had broken their covenant with Him.

But there was something else going on. Yes, God set out to destroy the pagans. Yes, the destruction of Jericho was complete and gruesome. But look at the grace God displayed up to the very last moment. Before God utterly destroyed Jericho, God gave the Canaanites living within the walls of Jericho one last chance to return to Him.

One last chance? Seven last chances, in fact.

The seven priests with the rams' horns marched in front of the Ark of the Lord, blowing their horns. Again the armed men marched both in front of the priests with the horns and behind the Ark of the Lord. All this time the priests were blowing their horns. On the second day they again marched around the town once and returned to the camp. **They followed this pattern for six days.**

On the seventh day the Israelites got up at dawn and marched around the town as they had done before. But this time they went around the town seven times. The seventh time around, as the priests sounded the long blast on their horns, Joshua commanded the people, "Shout! For the Lord has given you the town! (Joshua 6:13-16, emphasis added).

The battle for Jericho was not a surprise attack. The people of Jericho knew the Jewish army and Jewish nation of several million people were camped just across the river. They had heard the stories of the other towns the Jewish army had battled and won. They knew an attack was coming.

What probably was a surprise was how the war was waged. God instructed the Jews to march around the walls of Jericho for seven days. Basically, God gave everyone in the city a 7-day opportunity to return to Him in faith.

God told Abraham that his descendants would become many nations (Genesis 17:6). He did not tell Abraham his descendants would become only the Jewish nation; but *many nations.* God included Gentiles also in that promise and, God fulfilled that promise by creating many nations through Abraham's son Ishmael. Ishmael's descendants included those Gentiles living in Jericho as well as many of us living today.

Genetics and lineage aside, when we come to faith in Jesus today, we spiritually come under the God's covenant with Abraham. As Paul tells us.

> ***Know then that it is those of faith who are the sons of Abraham.*** *And the Scripture, foreseeing that God would justify the Gentiles by faith, preached the gospel beforehand to Abraham, saying, "In you shall all the nations be blessed." So then, those who are of faith are blessed along with Abraham, the man of faith* (Galatians 3:7-9, emphasis added).

This is Rahab's story. She recognized clearly that, once she chose to believe in God, He granted her His grace. He saved her because of her faith, rather than pour out justice against her.

When we recognize that we have received God's grace and when we live with gratitude for it, we understand how God might see His women of faith. We can respond:

I am like Rahab.

For Thought and Discussion

- What does it mean to you to have God's grace?

- What types of favor do you see that God has granted you personally in your life?

- Is there an area of God's favor that you don't feel you have yet received? Or have not asked for? What is stopping you from asking and receiving?

PRAYER: Dear Jesus, thank you for your grace when we don't deserve it. Thank you for your favor upon us. We know we don't deserve your favor, so please help us remember to be grateful for it in all things. Amen.

Day 25—I Know God is in Heaven

*When we heard of it, our hearts melted in fear and everyone's courage failed because of you, for **the Lord your God is God in heaven above** and on the earth below* (Joshua 2:11).

One of my favorite parts of the Lord's Prayer is reciting, *thy will be done on earth as it is in heaven.* What I love about that line is the recognition that God's will is done in heaven—always; every moment; without question. Heaven is perfect. It is perfect because God is there and He is in charge. His will is done in heaven always.

Although God is in ultimate control, sometimes it is hard to see His hand down here on earth. Today let's focus on heaven, because even though evil abounds on earth and God's will is sometimes thwarted, it's reassuring to remember that, no matter what is happening down here, God is in complete control in heaven. Since we believers will end up in heaven one day, that's an awesome truth to hold on to.

When Rahab first met the Jewish spies, she acknowledged God's power. She acknowledged that God was in control, saying "the Lord your God is God in heaven above."

Most ancient pagan religions, such as the ancient Egyptians and Babylonians, believed in an afterlife. The people who worshipped those pagan gods believed they would have a life better than on this earth—like our concept of heaven. Rahab, brought up in a pagan society would have understood the concept of heaven. For her to believe that our God—the God of the Jewish people—was the Lord in heaven, was a huge statement of faith.

Things were different in Old Testament times. Yes, angels visited from time to time, as did "pre-incarnate Jesus" (when the Lord God showed up in human form). The Holy Spirit was also present in a few people's lives, usually temporarily and God the Father was with Moses on the mountaintop.

But as a general rule, the ancient Jewish people believed God's presence was in the Ark of the Covenant within the Most Holy Place in the Temple. Otherwise, they believed God, spent His time in heaven. They believed He was seated on His throne in heaven, overseeing things, sending angels here and there, making sure His plan was accomplished, that the stars all stayed in place and the planets continued to spin.

Later, God the Son—Jesus—came to live on earth and after His return to heaven, the Holy Spirit came to stay here with all of us who believe in Jesus the Christ. But it is in heaven where God's true kingdom is, referred to by Jesus again and again as the "Kingdom of Heaven."

In fact, when Jesus taught His disciples how to pray, He specified to ask that "thy will (God's) be done, on earth *as it is in heaven*" (Matthew 6:10). Jesus' prayer instructions confirm that God's will is done in heaven. Always. God is God in heaven.

If heaven is where God is and where He is making and implementing His plans, we should feel special confidence. We don't know the details of God's plans. We certainly can't fully understand them. But we can learn enough about God's character through reading Scripture, through our relationship with Jesus and through the leading of the Holy Spirit, that we know God is good. Therefore His plan—whatever that plan is—is good. God, the good Father can't make a plan that isn't good.

Therefore we have confidence. We have joy. We have peace. God is in control. God is seated on His throne in heaven. "The Lord your God is the God in heaven above," said Rahab.

This is Rahab's story. She acknowledged that the God the Jews worshipped was the Lord in heaven above.

When we realize the truth and remember it—that God is in perfect control of everything in heaven above, regardless of what is happening here on earth, we understand how God might see His women of faith. We can respond,

I am like Rahab.

For Thought and Discussion

- What assurance do you feel when you recite *The Lord's Prayer* acknowledging that God's will is being done in heaven? How does that assurance give you encouragement for what is happening down here?

- Has there ever been a time when you prayed for one thing and God's will was clearly different and better? What did you learn from that experience?

- What specific things should you be praying for God's will rather than your own ideas of how things should be done?

PRAYER: Dear Jesus, thank you for reminding us to keep praying that God's will be done here on earth just like it is always being done in heaven. Help us always keep the focus on your will regardless of what we might think should happen. Help us to pray for your will in all situations, knowing it is perfect. Amen.

Day 26—I Know God is on Earth

ॐ৵

*When we heard of it, our hearts melted in fear and everyone's courage failed because of you, for **the Lord your God is God** in heaven above and **on the earth below** (Joshua 2:11).*

Yesterday we were reminded that God the Father is in heaven. He is right there with Jesus making sure His plan—His good and perfect plan—is being accomplished. We know that whatever His plan is, it is good and therefore we can have peace and trust in Him.

What's hard for us is to look around at what is happening here on earth and know that God's will is not being done everywhere. The most we sometimes can hope for is that we understand God's will for our own lives and work to see that happen.

What we can also be encouraged by though is that after Jesus died, was resurrected and returned to heaven, He left the Holy Spirit behind. The Holy Spirit—the third part of the Trinity of Father, Son, and Spirit—used to make an appearance from time to time before Jesus lived His earthly life. Those times were occasional and sometimes they were temporary.

Once Jesus returned to heaven though, He sent the Holy Spirit. We don't have to do a thing on our own to receive the Spirit—simply surrender our lives to Jesus and the gift of God Himself in our lives is ours.

Now, admittedly we don't always allow ourselves to sense the leading of the Spirit or we stop listening. That's our inability. The Spirit is still there, ready, waiting, eager to help us live our lives for Jesus. We can't ask for more of the Holy Spirit. We have all of Him at all times. We can't have more or less. We get all of God. Rather, it's a matter of how much of God can we handle? Are we able to only allow the Spirit to be our inner conscience? Or are we able to allow the Spirit to speak through us in words we don't understand ourselves? Or are we at a point where we sense the Spirit leading us at some level in between?

Wherever we are on our journey of faith, the fact remains that the Holy Spirit is with us. The Holy Spirit is here on earth, living in us and working through us when we allow Him to.

Rahab's statement of faith to the Jewish spies included her understanding that the Lord "is God on the earth below." She had heard the stories. She knew about the plagues God had sent to the Egyptians when the Jews tried to leave Egypt. She knew how the Red Sea had parted when the Jews fled across it. She had heard the stories about Abraham, Isaac, Israel and Ishmael, who may have been her own ancestors. Now she was seeing God's army camped just outside her city walls. She knew God's power. She knew, right then when she first professed her faith that the Lord is God on earth; just as He is God in heaven too.

Jesus taught us to pray the request that "thy will be done on earth as it is in heaven." God is God in heaven above and here on earth also.

This is Rahab's story. She recognized that the God of the Jews was Lord of heaven above. She recognized that He was also Lord of earth below.

When we recognize the truth that Rahab knew, that whatever happens, God is still Lord, even when situations feel out of control, we understand how God might see His women of faith. We can respond:

I am like Rahab.

For Thought and Discussion

- Although God allows bad things to happen, He can still make good come out of bad things. How does this give you an understanding of His power and love?

- Despite whatever else is happening around us, we can—like Rahab—remember that God is Lord. In what ways can you remember God's divine nature, His love and His plan to encourage you when things do not feel as if they are happening according to your expectation?

- How can you better attune yourself to the Holy Spirit's leading? In what ways will sensing the Holy Spirit help you remember that God is here on earth with you?

PRAYER: Dear Jesus, thank you for living on earth so that we have your example of how to live. Thank you for leaving the Holy Spirit with us so that your power is available to us at every moment. Holy Spirit, please help us sense and follow your leading so that we can be reminded that you are Lord here on earth. Amen.

Day 27—I Listen for the Trumpet

My dad loved Dixieland jazz. His favorite artist was Louis Armstrong. We'd watch Louie play on the *Ed Sullivan Show*, white handkerchief in one hand, belting out the jazz. Mid note, he'd wipe the sweat off his brow and keep playing.

Mom on the other hand, loved Herb Alpert and the Tijuana Brass band of trumpeters. They could take any song and turn it into something you could dance to.

No doubt Rahab was also fond of trumpets; because trumpets signaled her salvation.

> *When the trumpets sounded, the army shouted, and at the sound of the trumpet, when the men gave a loud shout, the wall collapsed; so everyone charged straight in, and they took the city* (Joshua 6:20).

The trumpet was one of the Israelite's most important musical instruments. Many Bible scholars think the trumpet played by the Jews marching around Jericho might have been a *shofar*, which was an instrument made from a ram's horn. The musician blew into one end and out came a loud note. Think conch shell horns in Hawaii. What was significant about the shofar was that blowing the shofar indicated God's presence and helped assure victory. Jericho was, in fact, a holy war.

> When you go into battle in your own land against an enemy who is oppressing you, sound a blast on the trumpets. Then you will be remembered by the Lord your God and rescued from your enemies (Numbers 10:9).

Imagine Rahab waiting for the battle for Jericho to begin. She must have kept an eye out her window constantly, looking for the Jewish army; wondering when they would attack. She might have wondered why they hadn't started building a mound to scale the walls. Or perhaps she expected a siege of another kind. She probably was *not* expecting the army to just march around the city tooting their horns and then leaving for the day; only to return the next day and do the same thing.

But after several days, Rahab probably began looking out her window, encouraged to see the army marching and hearing those trumpets again, even though she hadn't seen the kind of battle she expected. Imagine the seventh day when Rahab heard the army marching around the city again; listened to the sound of their feet hitting the hard ground. She knew the trumpets would be played again.

After the trumpets ended, maybe there was a moment of silence as Rahab waited for the army to leave again as they had each day. But instead of leaving, all of the Jewish soldiers shouted together. The shouting filled the air. Rahab felt the city walls shudder. Perhaps her oil lamp fell to the floor and broke. A baby next door began to whimper. A woman screamed. The livestock began to panic.

Then as Rahab looked out the window at the homes near hers, she saw the great walls of Jericho crack and crumble around her. She must have had a moment of panic and doubt. Would she have looked out the window, expecting to see Jewish soldiers raising a ladder to her window for her escape? Did she wonder if they would remember her at all? With the wall crumbling, had she further endangered her family by bringing all of them into her home built in the wall? Rahab would have needed extra faith during that moment to wait patiently for deliverance, while keeping her frightened family together.

When the Jewish army arrived at Rahab's house, she recognized that the trumpets had been a signal—to the army, to the people of Jericho and to her. The city fell literally and militarily. All that remained was for the Jewish army to rescue Rahab and her family and take them to safety. Those trumpets had signaled her salvation.

Trumpets will signal our salvation also.

Then the seven angels who had the seven trumpets prepared to sound them (Revelation 8:6).

Just prior to Jesus' return, seven angels will be given seven trumpets. Each of the first six trumpets will sound before a plague or catastrophe will occur on earth.

The first trumpet signals hail and fire to burn up grass and trees on earth (Revelation 8:7).

The second trumpet signals a burning object that is thrown into the oceans turning them to blood and destroying one third of sea life and ships (verses 8-9).

The third trumpet signals a burning star falling into fresh water causing it to become bitter and kill many people (verses 10-11).

The fourth trumpet signals the diminishing of the light by the sun, moon and stars by one third (verse 12).

The fifth trumpet signals five months of stinging locusts (Revelation 9:1-12).

The sixth trumpet signals four angels to kill one-third of the earth's remaining population (verses 13-19).

Those catastrophes are horrifying. But there is a seventh trumpet to come. The final trumpet signals praise and worship. It is followed by a great battle and final judgment, but it signals the opening of God's temple in heaven and reminds us that what is to come is very good.

> *The seventh angel sounded his trumpet, and there were loud voices in heaven, which said:*
>
> *"The kingdom of the world has become the kingdom of our Lord and of his Messiah, and he will reign for ever and ever."* (Revelation 11:15).

This is Rahab's story. She heard the trumpet sound and knew her rescue was at hand. Then she joined the Israelites, their God becoming her God; their faith becoming hers.

When we remember that Jesus will signal His return with music of trumpets and rejoice in His salvation, we understand how God might see His women of faith. We can respond:

I am like Rahab.

For Thought and Discussion

- Music is spoken of in Scripture often in relationship to worship. Do you have a favorite verse about music? Why is it meaningful to you?

- Think of the imagery of heralds in medieval times, blowing their trumpets to announce the king. How do those images influence your thinking about Jericho? About Jesus' return?

- Throughout the New Testament, Jesus tells people that we won't know when He will return but that we should be ready for that day. Are you ready? In what way do you need to prepare? How do you remain faithful?

PRAYER: Dear Jesus, thank you for sound and music. Thank you for reminding us through Joshua and Rahab that your power can be seen in many ways. Please open our eyes and ears and help us find your power each day. Amen.

Day 28—I am Rahab

Afriend shared the story of her father who had refused to let Jesus be his Lord. Then on the man's deathbed, he accepted Jesus, was forgiven and is now assured of heaven. Many of us have stories like this of our own. Scripture tells us that God is patient, not wanting to lose anyone but for everyone to join His family. Even at the last moment.

> *The Lord is not slow in keeping his promise, as some understand slowness. Instead he is patient with you, not wanting anyone to perish, but everyone to come to repentance* (2 Peter 3:9).

When we meet Rahab, we see the Jewish people entering the Promised Land. They have just spent 40 years wandering in the desert. As they camp next to the city of Jericho, the Jews are at the end of their wandering; ready to move forward with God.

Rahab joined God's family late in the game. God always wanted to include everyone in His plan of salvation. The inclusion of Rahab (a Canaanite) and Ruth (a Moabite) in Jesus' genealogy is an indication that God intended everyone to be part of His family—not just the Jewish people but the Gentiles (non-Jews) as well.

God wants our love to be freely given to Him, however, thus He allows free will, which means we have to choose Him. Rahab did. Jesus told His disciples that He came first to save the Jews. Jesus Himself was born into a Jewish family. The Jews were God's chosen. He loved all of His creations, including us Gentiles, but He had a special place in His heart for the Jews.

Fortunately for us, Jesus also came to save us, even though—as the Canaanite woman refers to the Gentiles—we are not sitting up at the banquet, but are the dogs under the table happy to have the scraps that fall.

> He (Jesus) *answered, "I was sent only to the lost sheep of Israel."*
>
> *The woman came and knelt before him. "Lord, help me!" she said.*
>
> *He replied, "It is not right to take the children's bread and toss it to the dogs."*
>
> *"Yes it is, Lord," she said. "Even the dogs eat the crumbs that fall from their master's table."*
>
> *Then Jesus said to her, "Woman, you have great faith! Your request is granted." And her daughter was healed at that moment* (Matthew 15:24-28, explanation added).

Coincidentally, the woman in the above verses talking with Jesus was a Canaanite woman. Like Rahab. Her point was that we Gentiles (non-Jews) came to the faith game late, too. But then God let us enter.

I am Rahab

We read a lot about grace in the New Testament. But lest we forget or fail to see, God's grace existed in the Old Testament too, despite a big focus on rules and regulations God had set up to help the Jewish people remain faithful to Him. What is different about the New Testament is that Jesus brought the law and grace back together and He brought all nations on earth that began from Abraham's line Abraham back together through Him. Now, not only the Jews are God's people. We spiritually also become part of Abraham's family.

One thing I love about names is that they mean something. The name Rahab was an Amorite name. Her people were pagan. They worshipped idols. Some scholars believe the first part of her name—Ra—refers back to the name of the main, number one Egyptian sun god. One of the meanings of the name Rahab is fierceness. When I look at the personality of Rahab, I see that, despite the possibility that her name referred to a pagan god, she exhibited the fierceness part of her character and became "all out" for the one true God.

Over the past 27 days, we have thought about how we live in a pagan society today, that there are spiritual walls which separate us from God and that there are also spiritual hedges which protect us. Our challenge is now:

In what way do I still feel separated from God? How can I pursue a deeper relationship with God so He can work more effectively in and through me?

We have also seen that there is a spiritual battle surrounding us but that it is God's battle. We can, however, participate in the battle, as part of God's team, being courageous and open to new ways to fight evil. Our challenge is now:

163

I am Rahab

How can I trust in God's victory and be proactive about fighting evil? How can my faith in Jesus give me strength and courage to do what is right?

We have recognized that we are sinners. We also saw that although God does not approve of lying in general, what may be more important is having a right relationship with others as a reflection of a right relationship with Him. We praise God that even though we are not righteous, He has decided to consider us so. We understand that God knows our past and loves us anyway and that our gratitude for His forgiveness results in a greater love for Him and others. Our challenge is now:

In what way does my understanding of my unworthiness and God's deep grace and mercy help me reach out to forgive and love others in His name?

We have recognized that God wants to use us to work at His plan. We know that God may be doing something completely new but that God sees us when we can help other people on God's team. Our challenge is now:

What might God be calling me to do—start a ministry, extend one or help with one already begun? What first step can I take toward allowing God to use me in a new way?

We have considered Rahab's scarlet cord and how it spiritually symbolizes the blood of Christ He shed on the cross. We recognize our need to display that scarlet cord for others to see, joining God's family, accepting His favor and working to bring others into His family. Our challenge is now:

In what ways is God leading me to evangelize? Who in my family and circle of friends and acquaintances does not know Jesus? What first step can I take to introduce them to Jesus?

We have focused on the truth that God is in control in heaven and that God will be victorious over evil one day. Until then, it is our job to remain faithful to Him, work fiercely to accomplish His plan and listen for the trumpet sound. Our challenge is now:

What can I do with this one and only earthly life to faithfully share Jesus with others? What do I need to do personally to remain faithful to Him?

The story of Rahab is the story of a changed life. She lived in a pagan society. She heard about the one true God and made the conscious decision to believe in Him, even though everyone around her did not. Then when push came to shove, Rahab confessed God to be the true, powerful Lord of heaven and earth and set out to live her faith, courageously leaving her people and joining God's family. She is remembered today as a heroine who participated in God's holy war and helped save His chosen people. Then God honored her by including her in the earthly genealogy of his one and only Son, Jesus.

This is Rahab's story. But when we understand that God has honored us by our decision to believe in Him, confessed our love for Him and acknowledged Him to be the true, powerful Lord of heaven and earth and have courageously set about living a life as part of His family, we understand how God might see His women of faith. We can respond.

I am like Rahab. In fact, in many ways, I *am* Rahab.

Love, Rahab

For Thought and Discussion

- In what ways might you have begun this study thinking poorly of Rahab because of her profession? Has that view changed?

- How does the story make you think differently about how God sees our sinful past in relation to where we are when we have joined His family?

- How does the story of Rahab make you consider your own life and what more you could do for God? What first step can you take to do so?

PRAYER: Dear Jesus, thank you for the lives of people recorded in Scripture. Thank you so much for including so many people who began their journey of faith in sin. Thank you for showing them such grace and mercy as a way of reminding us that your grace and mercy is there for us, too. Amen.

Other studies in the

With Faith Like Hers series

available or coming soon:

I am Eve

I am Esther

I am Ruth

I am Mary (Jesus' mother)

I am Elizabeth

I am Rahab

I am Hannah

I am Deborah

Resources

Be sure to visit the author at CarolPetersonAuthor.com.

If you enjoyed this study, please let others know. One of the best ways to let folks know is to leave a review. Just go to Amazon.com, find the title of this book and click on "Write a Customer Review." Thanks in advance!

Sources

Bailey, Kenneth E. *Jesus Through Middle Eastern Eyes: Cultural Studies in the Gospels.* IVP Academic, Downers Grove, IL, 2009.

Biblegateway.com is a fabulous online resource. It provides a quick and easy way to read the same Scripture in various versions for deeper understanding. It also has quite good commentaries that encourage a desire to find out more.

Deen, Edith. *All of the Women of the Bible.* San Francisco: Harper San Francisco, 1983. [Interesting for a general overview of women in Scripture.]

Glo Interactive Bible. Immersion Digital, LLC, 2009. [Great resource for background and historical information about people and places in Scripture.]

Interpreter's Bible; The Holy Scriptures in the King James and Revised Standard Versions with General Articles and Introduction, Exegesis, Exposition for Each Book of the Bible. New York: Abingdon Press, 1952. [This 12-volume Bible belonged to my Pastor dad who purchased them during or shortly after seminary. He used them for 45 years of sermon preparation. Now they're my first go-to when I need solid, theological commentary or explanation.]

The New Strong's Concise Concordance of the Bible. Nashville: Thomas Nelson, 2005. [Helpful to understand meaning of original words in Scripture and locating passages.]

OpenBible.info is another good online resource. I love the site's ability to search based on a word or topic. Although the results sometimes feel computer generated (because they are!) it's still a good place to start expanding a line of thinking.

Vine, W.E. *Vine's Complete Expository Dictionary of Old and New Testament Words.* Nashville: Thomas Nelson Publishers, 1996. [Helpful in understanding the meaning of the original words in Scripture.]

Zondervan NIV Study Bible. Grand Rapids: Zondervan, 2002. [Good, basic study notes for quick overview of Scripture.]

The best and most valuable source—always—is prayer, study and God's leading. It's easy and tempting to come up with personal theology and proclaim it brilliant. It's harder, but always best, to rely on God's leading and to check any "personal brilliance" against the truth of God's Word set forth in Scripture.

From the Author

I was raised in a Christian home—the daughter of a Protestant minister. But it wasn't until I was in my late twenties that I took full ownership of my faith and began the long process of learning what it means to be a Christian and a child of God. I'm still learning.

When I began writing for publication, I was blessed by early publishing success when my first four books were picked up by a respected educational publisher. My mission became to write in a way that would educate, inspire and entertain others.

Gradually I moved from writing for children to writing for young women and—more recently—to writing for women seeking to deepen their faith in Christ. Someone in the writing world once said that "all writing is basically autobiographical." That's true for me as I write this Bible study series. I seek to understand and deepen my own faith as I write to help other women understand and deepen theirs.

I live in Idaho with my husband of more than 35 years. I have two grown children who taught me that if God only loves me a fraction of how much I love them— wow, God loves me a lot!

Made in the USA
Middletown, DE
20 September 2022

10279555R00106